"I think that this is a renaissance book! I was deeply moved by your experiences of God's grace."
"This is a beautifully written narrative of the lives of two prayer-partners and the people in the larger circle of their lives. We are invited into a journey of faith, of friendships, of healing, and best of all of the unfolding discovery of the love and faithfulness of Jesus Christ.
It is also a realistic and quietly told story of the meaning and experiences of prayer. As I read, I realized that I was being led into a living school of prayer and by teachers who were in no way self serving or self focused. Their eyes are on Christ; this makes all the difference - for the teachers and the taught.
Jeff Ayers is a skillful teller of their journey and I recommend this book."

--Earl F. Palmer, Earl Palmer Ministries

"A compelling, inspirational, and unusual story of two unlikely partners in prayer who have spent 35 years praying together and, through their ministry, touching the lives of many. Read and be encouraged!"

--Denny Rydberg
President, Young Life

"Here is a wonderfully frank and personal account of friendship, prayer, and the persistent faithfulness of our loving Savior. From the beginning Ruth's story and Tom's story draw us into God's story. Alive to Jesus in the challenges of everyday life, they and their circle of friends discover life as a bold adventure of faith. If you're like me, this book will make you ask: Who has God put in my life? And how soon can we get started in prayer?"

-- George Hinman, Senior Pastor, University Presbyterian Church

"Ruth and Tom read that Jesus said to his followers, "…ask in my name…." (John 14:13-14). Jesus also said, "For where two or more are gathered in my name, I am there among them." (Matthew 18:20) Those Biblical realities helped Ruth and Tom pray together as partners in ministry for over 35 years and along the way they discovered the awesome power of prayer comes not only from the answers to their prayers, but in the praying itself. I have been blessed in knowing them, their incredible stories, their faithful friends, and the amazing joy of praying "in his name."

--Ray Moore, Pastor of Congregational Care, University Presbyterian Church

"This is a powerful story of two people who not only believe in the power of prayer, but who have experienced it in their individual lives and in their prayer ministry together. You will be encouraged in your own prayer life as you read their witness to the amazing things that God has done in and through them."

--Bob Davies, Worship Dept., University Presbyterian Church, Seattle

"In the times of my hopelessness, I relied on the prayer partnership between my Aunt Ruth and "cousin" Tom. Through God's grace their prayers became a source of my strength and dedication to serve the Lord. I continually thank God for their presence in my life, and I am confident that their words will inspire their readers."

--Lily Mationg, Family Relative in CA

In His Name:
A 35-Year Prayer Partnership

By
Ruth Vega-Norton and Tom Grime

AS TOLD TO
Jeff Ayers

Copyright © 2002-2011 by Ruth Vega Norton and Tom Grime
All rights reserved

Without limiting the rights under copyright reserved above, no part of this publication may be reproduced, stored in or introduced into a retrieval system, or transmitted, in any form, or by any means (electronic, mechanical, photocopying, recording, or otherwise), without the prior written permission of the copyright owners.

The scanning, uploading, and distribution of this book via the Internet or via any other means without the permission of the publisher is illegal and punishable by law. Please purchase only authorized electronic editions, and do not participate in or encourage electronic piracy of copyrighted materials. Your support of the author's rights is appreciated.

ISBN: 1461040701

ISBN-13: 9781461040705

"To Our Lord, the Author and Finisher of our Faith.
To you this book belongs!
Author and Finisher of our partnership also,
that others may know...Amen."

(Ruth's prayer for the book)

Cover Photo

Courtesy of Erica Browne Grivas of My Green Lake, a Seattle Green Lake blog. This Green Lake bench and garden was dedicated to Josefa Barrazona in 2000 and is located around the walking path at Green Lake.

Acknowledgments

We wish to thank the special people who during the last ten years helped us write this book.

For Bob Davies who first encouraged us to write this book, to document and inspire other people to the power of partnered praying.

We would gratefully like to thank Maria Meredith for her early work in 2000 to begin to gather and write for the book…

And for Deborah Anderson's hard work to interview, record and write the stories found in the book.

Special thanks to Pastor Ray Moore for his timely direction, encouragement, and inspiration…

A God-given friend, John O'Melveny Woods (author of "Return to Treasure Island") whom we met on a San Diego to Seattle airplane flight. He offered us encouragement, inspiration, and kindness when we needed it most. You graciously and patiently answered our questions of what to do next!

And lastly, for our dear friend Jeff Ayers, who brought everything together through his many skills as a writer and author.

Proceeds from the sale of this book go to support On Eagle's Wings Foundation, a non-profit foundation based in Seattle, Washington that supports youth entrepreneurial development and low-cost access to training and discipleship in the Philippines.

This book is dedicated to:

Josefa Encarnation Diaz Barrazona

Ruth's mom and Tom's adopted grandmother.
She was featured in the book,
Washington Women as Path Breakers
by Mildred T. Andrews

Contents

ONE	Ruth's Early Years	1
TWO	Ruth's Arrival in America	39
THREE	Tom Grime	49
FOUR	Ruth and Tom's Life of Prayer	63
FIVE	Ruth and Tom's Prayer Relationship	99
SIX	Ruth and Tom's Prayer Relationship Plus One	113
SEVEN	God is Good	127

Their story sang to me when I first heard it. Ruth Vega-Norton, a woman from the Philippines now living in the United States, and Tom Grime, a man from a troubled childhood trying to find his way in life, drew each others name out of a hat and became prayer partners and have continued to pray for over 35 years. They are still together now even though Ruth has married. With her husband and Tom's help, they created a non-profit foundation to help others back in the Philippines find housing, food, and a sense of entitlement.

We go to the same church in Seattle, University Presbyterian and though I had seen them both regularly, I had no idea their history together or separate until I heard them talking about a book. Both friends and acquaintances had suggested they write a book, but they didn't know how to proceed. They had a woman help them organize their thoughts, but at the end, it didn't work out. As I talked to Ruth and Tom more, I realized that I felt compelled to tell their story and I wanted to write it. With their blessing and amazing honesty in answering my questions, I set to work.

In the end, this is their story, told by them, starting with Ruth as a little girl growing up in a war torn country...

From the moment Ruth Vega-Norton was born, she proved herself to be a force in the work of the Lord. As she grew up and lived in different parts of the world, she experienced joy and tragedy that would easily shake her faith in others. Instead, it reinforced her belief in the Lord's constant love. A small woman whose commanding presence can still dominate a room, she has spent her entire life proving to even the skeptical that the power of prayer works and can change lives. Here is her story and the story of several people whose lives changed as a result of her efforts.

ONE
RUTH'S EARLY YEARS

"To our Lord, the Author and Finisher of our faith.
To you this book belongs!
Author and Finisher of our prayer partnership also,
that others may know." Amen
Hebrews 12:2

Josefa Encarnacion Diaz Barrazona, my mother, had experienced much tragedy by the time I came into the world. She lived in the Philippines and the Flu Epidemic of 1918 cut her first marriage short. Tragically two of her four children and her husband died as a result of the sickness, leaving her a widow with two small children, a boy and a girl. So when an opportunity to study in America at the Deaconess Training School in the Pacific Northwest became available, she arranged for her two surviving children to be cared for by her mother in law and headed for America. She was a life-long Methodist and hoped to learn the qualities of being a better mother and provide for her children. Once she arrived in the Pacific Northwest and was settled, she sent for her children. Her mother in law allowed only her son to join her.

Josefa Encarnacion Diaz Barrazona (front, right). This was her graduation from missionary school photo.

While attending school in the U.S., she met and married my father, a town mate from the Philippines. The July 1924 issue of the Philippine Republic called him, "the Filipino Billy Sunday." The article described him as an "evangelist...(addressing) great crowds (who) won and personally baptized many converts in a series of revival meetings...across the United States." He was quite the charismatic leader.

When my mother's training in missionary work ended, it seemed that God had brought the two of them together for a life of ministry. As they began their work for the Lord, she gave birth to a little girl who died shortly afterwards. Battling grief, they continued on in their ministry.

Soon after, my mother became pregnant again; this time with me. When it came time for my delivery into the world, the doctor was late in arriving. The nurse used the palm of her hand to try to stop me from coming out, but I insisted. Enter with boldness.... Ruth Diaz Vega Norton. I was named Ruth in honor of the principal of the Deaconess School of whom my mother had respect. Shortly after I came into the world, my parents gave me a baby brother. It looked like life was going to get better.

There was a young girl, brought in as a nanny to help with housework and help raise the kids. One day while she was ironing, my mother noticed that her tummy was getting big. She asked and discovered that she was pregnant. The guilty culprit? My dad. He had, as the expression goes, fallen from Grace. My mom threw him out. Bundling us up with some of her belongings, we returned to the Philippines, leaving my father behind. Years later, when I finally saw my dad again, he told me the last memory he had of our family was me in the window, waving goodbye. My mom told me that shortly after being thrown out, my dad came back to get our nanny and she said, "No. I don't want to go with you." That was when my mom realized that she was probably forced into sex with him.

In the Philippines, a while after we had settled, an odd postcard arrived: On the front was a picture of a woman and a man caressing, and a baby not far away, emotionless, naked, with it's tummy in a shallow lake. On the back was written one word in Tagalog "Paalam na", Good-bye.

This is the postcard they received.

The fall from Grace was long and hard.

Much to my amazement, my mother eventually took the nanny and her child in and helped her a great deal. When I asked my mom how she could do such a thing, she said, "It was all the easier to forgive, knowing the pregnancy was not her choice."

The postcard remained a mystery eventually ending up in my possession as a reminder of what can happen when a person loses the focus of the Lord's call and falls into disobedience.

I was two years old when we returned to the Philippines; the Methodist mission post Nueva Ecija Girls' Dormitory in Cabanatuan became the world in which I was immersed. In the central plains of the Island of Luzon, this soon became my sanctuary; my mother's place of service.

Josefa dressed in Filipina costume; second row, 2nd from the right. Ruth is in the middle of the first row.

In the Philippines, high schools were only in the capital cities of the various provinces. There were no high schools in the small towns. That is why the Methodists mission established dormitories and to whom my mom was responsible. She always took me with her.

I lived with the girls going to high school in the dormitories. As if I was a cherished cherub, everyone doted on me; the older girls who lived there; aunts, uncles, my grandmother and the missionaries who administered the school. Even the cook would protect me should anyone threaten me with harm, even from my mom when I disobeyed many times. With a smile that rarely dimmed, my adventurous spirit flourished in the safety of such an enriched environment.

I was a reader from an early age. The second and third grade teachers would have me read to the class and then have me go to other classes and read while my class would be learning arithmetic. To this day, I'm terrible at math.

Looking back, I can see my natural love of the work of the Lord as I gathered the neighborhood children around to 'play prayer'. Solemnity gave way to giggles as we experimented with speaking and praying in English, ending up with our own version of speaking in tongues.

All playing aside, I discovered I loved prayer. I loved the knowledge of God's presence in my own life and the lives of those around me. At the age of twelve, I committed my life to the Lord at a revival meeting of the Pilgrim Holiness church. A yearning for aspiring to obedience began. It was a gift placed inside me from the beginning.

Proverbs 28:9 is a verse that has great weight for me. "If anyone turns a deaf ear to the law, even his prayers are detestable." I firmly believe there is a connection between how we live our life and the flow of the Holy Spirit, not only because of my father's life but what has been true for me.

In those days, living in a third world, dorm life was relatively easy. There was always an abundance of food. Surrounded by a neighborhood in need, I would help my mother distribute the, sometimes still warm, leftovers from the dorm to the poor around us. We climbed up a ladder to pass them over the fence that enclosed the mission, and then we ministered to people, sharing generously all that was supplied for us. My mother's first impulse was always to give to others. Her works also extended beyond the fence helping any and all in need. The love between my mother and I was so strong, these acts of charity infused my heart with a similar pulse. I delighted in accompanying her on what my mom considered daily mercy trips.

Sometimes our excursions involved mortician's duties. My mother would prepare the bodies for burial, for the poor could not afford the arrangements. Carefully and lovingly she bathed each deceased under my watchful eye.

I remember a time when we arrived before the person died. In all my devotion to the Lord, I looked into their eyes and, as if I was many years older instead of so young, I reverently told them they needed to ask the Lord Jesus into their heart and invited them to do so. This helped grow a passion for evangelism with my developing faith. Everyday, in every way, I grew in the shadow of those who were seeking the Lord. I grew committed to serving him, and living our faith by passing it on to others, and I took the examples around me as my own.

Occasionally it was necessary for me to be left behind at the dormitory while my mother went on a visit. Howling inconsolably, my caregiver would play records of the Grand Operas on our Victorola phonograph, the only comfort for me. It was soothing. Only nestled in the glory of arias, like *Troubadour*, was I content to remain. It was a love that would foreshadow many musical endeavors as an adult.

Not only the faith, but also the moral battles of those nearby influenced me. I saw humanity at its worst and saw God's redemptive power in the willingness of my mother to call people to higher ground.

I remember my mother's reaction to a younger uncle who strayed from marital vows. Clutching my hand under the shade of an umbrella carried to ward off the hot sun, my mother traipsed far from town to a little hut. With all the strength of leadership and willingness to take a stand, Mom called loudly for my uncle to show his face. Sheepishly he appeared. "Carmella", she called to the woman, "Come out here!" As had the uncle, she came into view.

She scolded him, "What are you doing? You've got family. You've got responsibilities. You've got children. Get back to town." Intimidated and unable to do otherwise under the authority of her voice, he returned to his family and begged forgiveness.

The indelible imprinting of observing my mom and her service to the Lord would show itself many times over in my life in the future. It set the standard for understanding the importance of the partnership of faith and works. Praying, ministering, being in fellowship with those who know God and telling of His presence to those who did not know Him was like my air to breathe. Living those opportunities was like breathing. So, serving the Lord came naturally from the beginning.

By school age, I was more comfortable without the constant companionship of my mother. Afternoon duties kept mom busy and I amused myself with my new friends. Raised in an open and loving Protestant Christian community, it did not occur to me there might be denominational differences. When my Roman Catholic friends trotted off to afternoon catechism lessons, I went right along with them.

Being Protestant in the Philippines at that time meant a life of discrimination. The pelting of stones on the galvanized roof of our church competed with our singing. When this harassment first began, the congregation would stop and pray for protection. When it became practically routine, we persisted by singing louder than ever before with the assurance in our hearts that God would protect us.

I was sometimes worried about being a young Protestant missionary's daughter attending Roman Catholic Catechism classes. If the nuns did know the truth, they said nothing. If they knew, they must have been happy for another convert to the fold. Whatever the earthly reason, it was clear the Lord wanted me in those classes. The classes were wonderful and I loved them.

As the sessions came to a close the children were instructed there would be a special ceremony. I did not hear that the girls were to wear white dresses and veils. Alone in my endeavor, I knew exactly what dress I would wear: my favorite red-flowered one! On the big day, I came to the church and took my first communion. I remember the delicious breakfast and then pictures were going to be taken. The nuns took me aside while that was happening, but I thought it was just because I was special. The whole event was just the kind I loved; Holy Fellowship. At the end of the day, I was a Catholic.

If a person looks carefully at one's history, it is possible to see how one event opens doors that enable the will of God to be carried through by a mere mortal. The unanticipated episode of confirmation as a Catholic played to God's purpose for my life on many levels.

Even early on in life, God's plan for me was apparent. My Catholic upbringing, and my mom's life and witness, taught me fellowship, how to minister, and even how to reach my own people. Being a Catholic was my bridge to pass over chasms; my dual citizenship also provided authority and the ability to share a prophetic voice to my ethnic culture.

Spiritually, it set a formative precedent for me to look across denominational boundaries to find the heart of God, to grow and serve. Since the Lord intended for my ministry to cut a broad path, it encouraged me to have a 'discipline of willingness' to willingly go where God opened the doors and where I was called.

Women suffrage burst into bloom in the early 1930s. Ready or not, the women of our town decided it was time for the city fathers to include city mothers as well. There was hardly anyone in town that did not know my mom. The women formed a new party and elected her to run as a member of the city council. On top of a makeshift platform made out of a carabao wagon, my mom learned to speak publicly. Traveling on horseback, she went to the far off villages urging everyone, especially the women, to vote. Often, I would tag along. Well, half the population of the town seemed to be related to her and the other half were either her close friends or members of the church. She won by a landslide.

In 1941, when I was 16, the horror of World War II began. After three hundred years of Spanish occupation, with both the Japanese and the Americans fighting over Philippine soil, the cry of the hearts of the people, and mine as well, was 'Why don't you just leave us alone?'

War on any soil is bitter and cruel. Ordinary citizens' lives become about the business of, at the very least, staying out of harm's way and hopefully staying alive over the long haul.

When I think of Monday, December 8, 1941, I immediately hear the music of John Philip Sousa. I can't remember exactly which one of the Sousa compositions was played that memorable day, but it was the unmistakable Sousa strain that is still etched in my memory. His music like "Semper Fideles," "Stars and Stripes Forever," and others. Why do the Sousa Marches have anything to do with the bombing of Pearl Harbor? Because music has been a large influence in my life and many of my life changing experiences are interspersed with certain pieces of music.

That fateful morning, started as every morning did. A few seconds after the bell rang; someone started hammering the piano to the precise rhythm of those Sousa marches. The students were programmed to line up in twos like robots. Although we didn't have a choice, I can remember being enthusiastic and pleasantly motivated to line up. I thought it was fun.

I can still hear and see the battered upright piano, with its top lid open, every molecule of the sound reverberating within the cement walls of the staircase. Bearing the weight of the pianist's pounding, we obeyed what it told us to do: Urge us to hurry on; up those arduous stairs.

Going up those steps wasn't as laborious that morning. Each of us, not being allowed to talk as we climbed, was still basking in the memory of a folk dance festival held over the weekend. "Bulaklakan" (Flowering fields) was a new dance we learned especially for that occasion. We competed with other provincial high schools in our "sayas" (Philippine costumes) that matched the garland of fresh flowers we carried.

Our first period class teacher Miss Alvarez was unusually late. So we welcomed the opportunity to talk about the festival. We discussed how everyone in the school had participated and how, true to the name of the folk dance, the entire field of the stadium seemed to sway to the rhythm of the dancing flowers. We had practiced for months and it appeared to be worth it. All of us were excited that we had won first prize in the interurban competition.

When Miss Alvarez finally arrived, she looked grave. She just got out of an emergency teachers' meeting that announced the Japanese had attacked Pearl Harbor. Since we were not familiar where Pearl Harbor was, we had an "on the spot" geography lesson. She kept telling us, as if to reassure herself, "There's nothing to worry about, we'll conduct business as usual." Nevertheless, the news created somewhat of a pall throughout the rest of the day.

The news came as a surprise for almost everyone in town, because rarely did a newspaper, or a magazine make its way into the area. Radios were beyond the means of most families. In addition, the electricity at that time was not dependable. Only Mayor Rigor could have possibly received the telegraph message from Manila.

Amazingly, my mom and her neighborhood friends were not surprised. Unbeknown to us, they had been staying up late into the night scanning the skies with their naked eyes watching for the nightly appearance of a comet.

Comets, as explained by the sages of our town, have been from the beginning of time nature's way of heralding a major event. One of these was the birth of Christ. To this day, this belief continues. Comets seem to appear prior to a war between great powers of the world or a catastrophe of some kind.

My mother and her neighborhood friends confidently assured us; we were not considered a great power of the World. The war probably wouldn't have any effect on our small world. A neighbor, Mrs. Pagdanganan, who had a stint in Hawaii as an Army Corps nurse, also established Hawaii was a great distance from us.

Disbelief and shock abounded when the Superintendent of Schools announced the closure of all schools. We learned that a state of emergency had been declared. All public employees were told to return to their hometowns.

All out of town students, employees and their families began the frantic packing of their belongings! A skeleton crew was all that was left in all government offices.

There were only two bus companies in the town, with schedules few and far between. Parents who heard the news by word of mouth came immediately. (Telegraph was the only communication besides the regular mail; the telephone was still unaffordable for private use.) Many arrived in horse drawn caretelas unable to understand the interruption of their children's education. Other parents came in jeeps.

The girls whose parents couldn't come to help them pack were the last ones to leave. I can still see the dazed look on their faces while gathering their belongings. They moved and acted mechanically, unable to grasp the reality of a war and the sudden turn of events.

It all happened so fast. Our home that once housed about 20 to 25 girls and women was suddenly quiet. All the girls I counted as sisters and family were gone! Our hired cook, Manang Sabel, was one of the last ones to leave reluctantly.

In their own unexpressive way, Manang Sabel, our cook and my Mom were like sisters. In spite of Manang Sabel's lack of education, my mother taught her how to read. Manang knew instinctively when to step in and take over the task of being a surrogate mother to me. She had been in our family since I was very young.

Siesta time would find her the only one awake in the maids' quarters orally reading the Bible. She hailed from Ilocos Norte, one of the farthest northern provinces of Luzon. She couldn't comprehend the gravity of the order to evacuate. She insisted on staying, she felt her place was with us.

I can still hear the drone of her Ilocano accent, when she would loudly read the Bible. Every time I would fry an egg, I would think about how much more I liked the way she made them. I was a "picky" eater. I disliked fish in any shape or form from an earlier traumatic incident when I had a fish bone lodged in my throat. My eggs had to be cooked in a special way, with the yolk broken and turned "over easy."

I couldn't understand why Manang Sabel had to leave too. Puzzled, I sat on one of the steps and thought to myself, "Will I ever see her and my friends again? I can't believe all this is happening."

I remember sitting on the steps feeling the emptiness inside me, when the faint smell of fresh paint triggered memories of the recent painting of our dormitory.

The painter had just completed his job and had gone home. I was proud that our home was one of the few homes that boasted of color. Almost all the houses in our town were drab and unpainted. The painter my mom hired had the reputation of being one of the finest craftsmen from a neighboring province. I remember watching him on top of a long ladder carefully highlighting with several hues of green and yellow the ornate scrolls under the eaves.

Our upright piano was also recently purchased for the dozen or so girls who eagerly took music lessons and I did also. Not a minute went by that someone was not sitting there. I was still hearing the lilting melody of one of my favorite tunes, Maria Elena. I had danced to it at our latest prom. Now it was hauntingly silent.

I slowly climbed the stairs to the large bedroom I shared with five other girls. Five beds were stripped of all bedding. I felt like crying, but no tears would come. I couldn't help noticing our lockers neatly lined up against the wall. My locker was the only one left closed. Five were left gaping open with nothing left but old shoes and trash. For the first time, I discovered the devastating feeling of loneliness!

There I was feeling eerie about being alone; reminiscing by myself, so I was relieved to find my Mom had arrived. She announced that she had sent word for my brother who was in college in Manila to come home. She could not get hold of my sister who was farther away in Nursing School in Baguio. It was all right, she consoled herself, her uncle was in that city and she should be safe there with him.

I heard my name being called. It was Anita Soriano, one of my friends who lived in the neighborhood. She wanted me to come out and play. Her older brother, Dwarding, soon joined us in a rhythm game. I still remember the name of the tune, "Perfidia".

To help keep us busy, a well meaning American missionary lady had started a class on arts and crafts. With my help, we were able to round up a few of my friends and some neighborhood kids, but the class immediately dwindled to just me. All the parents wanted their children home.

Meantime, my Mom attended frequent Council meetings as a council member to discuss emergency measures and pass bills to prepare us for the unknown future.

Every neighborhood was urged to build bomb shelters. We were taught how to "blackout" our windows, and were required to participate in mock air raid drills. Non perishables such as canned food, grains, and dried fish and meat became prime commodities. Those who could afford it went on a hoarding binge.

Then one day the inevitable happened, our first air raid signal became a reality. We ran to our half finished bomb shelter. As soon as we were all inside, we heard cries and pounding on the roof. Two men came in with shrapnel wounds, bleeding profusely. It took all of us to calm them down and dress their wounds.

Our homes were left intact by the bombing, but our water supply was cut off. It was then we realized that one of the targets was our water reservoir.

As I mentioned before, radios were not affordable by many of the townspeople so news traveled by word of mouth. We learned that a Japanese Jujitsu instructor who lived in our neighborhood suddenly disappeared. In the outskirts of town was a military camp. People came to the conclusion that he must have been a spy. They began to remember the secrecy in how he arrived in our town disguised as a jujitsu instructor. We realized that no one had really gotten to know him nor did anyone know about his comings and goings.

One morning we woke up to the sound of caravans of people evacuating. We asked some of them where they were headed for and surprisingly, many did not actually know where they were going. Most just wanted to get out of town and go into hiding. Ready or not, my Mom and our neighbors, the Sorianos, decided in desperation that they didn't want to be left behind.

It was pretty grim seeing the population of our town dwindle down. The people on the move stayed off the main highway where the Japanese army was known to be raping and massacring civilians.

A tremendous force of foresight inspired my mother the night before we fled. Our dormitory had a concrete porch that measured approximately 30 x 30 ft. The concrete was hollow inside and had a small opening that faced away from the street. She decided this would be a good hiding place for our valuables, which we wouldn't be able to carry with us. So, she hid our silverware, china, old photographs, books, keepsakes and even clothes in that small space.

The town that was usually crowded with students and their activities began to look like a ghost town. Christmas, the most celebrated holiday in the Philippines with lavish preparations of hand made colorful lanterns, new attires, and gifts came and went without fanfare.

My Mom and our neighbors, the Sorianos, couldn't make up their minds where the safest place was to evacuate, so we lost several days dilly-dallying. One of our other neighbors still there, Tata Ito, decided to get ready anyway. He ordered one of his carts and a carabao brought to town from his farm. We loaded our few belongings and my Mom filled up the cart with food left over from our dormitory supplies.

We were piling in the last of our food when a fleet of army trucks loaded with Filipino soldiers, obviously in retreat, drove through town. The last truck in the convoy came to an abrupt halt in front of us. The one in command got off the truck and told the adults, "Be sure to watch out for your women, especially the young ones. The Japanese soldiers are raping every young woman they come across. Stay out of their way." Then they sped off leaving a cloud of dust behind them. Before the trucks faded into the distance, he quickly yelled, "It's best to travel at night, lay low in the daytime."

The time to act had come. It didn't matter whether we had enough food in our cart or a destination in mind. As soon as someone found a pair of scissors, our parents suddenly turned into accomplished barbers. They gave my girl friends and I boys' haircuts. Then they dressed us in borrowed boys' clothes and we left, not knowing our final destination. The warning from the soldier was enough and staying in town was the last thing we should do.

We traveled on foot all night long, stopping only to ask for directions to my Mom's sister's farm. In the light of the hazy full moon, it seemed so low, that we could almost touch it. People walked in pairs or threes behind their carts, some carrying babies in arms and children holding on to their mother's skirts. It looked so unreal, like in a slow motion movie. No one was talking, and when they did, all one could hear were whispers. None of the babies or children cried or fussed. Some of the adults moved as if walking in their sleep.

Once in a while, we would come across a group of people hunched over, eating food cooked over a campfire. They were willing to share their food with us and other passing, hungry strangers. That night, even if we didn't have the advantage of a full moon due to the cloud cover, I felt and saw the deep caring by everyone, even strangers, during this time. The imminent danger had bonded us together. Strangers became instant neighbors and families.

By daybreak, we finally reached my aunt's farm, completely exhausted from lack of sleep. My aunt, Ating, made breakfast ready for us. She begged us to stay in hiding with her, but the Sorianos persuaded my Mom to leave with them to the hills where we were assured it would be safer. We spent the day sleeping, grateful to have a reprieve from the air raid sirens and bombing in the city.

Later in the afternoon, some neighboring farmers pleasantly surprised us with baskets loaded with tomatoes, eggplants, and other vegetables. They wanted to know if we could use some of them. Harvest season was at its peak and they were blessed with a good crop that year. Engaging smiles were a proof of the Biblically time tested adage: "how more blessed it is to give than to receive." Modern refrigeration was of course still non-existent. Almost everyone was on the run and the farmers were delighted their produce would be used before they spoiled.

We decided to spend the next night at Ating's farm to regain our strength. She let us stay in one of the bamboo huts in the middle of her tobacco field. Before going to bed, making sure it was dark enough for us not to be seen, my Mom announced so that everyone within earshot could hear, that we were going into the middle of the field to relieve ourselves.

With the huge tobacco leaves shielding us from the others, and the light of the full moon bathing us as if it were daylight, she showed me the hem of the long skirt she was wearing. Inside the fold, she had me run my fingers to feel paper currency she had sewn inside. She informed me that the money was 100 and 500 peso bills. Then, she showed me a large glass jar filled with silver currency and heirloom jewelry that was encased in a pouch. With a stick, she started digging a hole large enough for the jar; then buried it safely for the night. She carefully showed me landmarks that made it easy for us to find it again. She explained that during the night our valuables would be safer there.

The next morning, before dawn, we went back to the same spot pretending to relieve ourselves again. We dug up our cache and waited for nightfall to resume our trek to the hills.

Again, the moon being our guide, we started for the unfamiliar terrain of the Penaranda hills. We found no path at all in the almost forest-like area.

As we reached this unknown territory, we began to hear staccato shots from automatic rifles. A salvo of tracer bullets suddenly crisscrossed the night sky! The acrid smell of gun smoke almost choked us, bringing tears to our eyes. We lay on the ground and tried to stay as low as possible. I still remember how bruised I was after it was over.

In the confusion, my Mom, brother, and I briefly got separated! As in a maze, we soon bumped into each other. My Mom immediately started ripping off the hem of her long skirt and started dividing money between my brother, and I, thinking we could be separated again. I'm sure she was also thinking she might be killed by a bullet in the surrounding skirmish.

I have no recollection of how we got to safety and away from the fighting. I just remember getting to an elevated part of the hill.

The next morning we found our traveling companions. The men had been scouting around and announced that they had found a safe place to set up camp.

We had survived the long night of crouching and creeping. The distant sounds of gunfire could now be barely heard and the familiar crowing of a rooster from a nearby farm reassured us like only an "all clear signal" could do.

We sat down under a tree exhausted from the ordeal. We began sharing our "nightmares" and our mutual fear for each other during the experience. The confusion between what was real and what was paranoia slowly came into perspective.

We could now pay attention to our body needs for food and other necessities. We began searching for our cart where all our supplies were stored. Our faithful carabao that was pulling our cart must have sensed the intensity of our need. She gave the loudest bellow I had ever heard from any animal of her kind. It must have been her own version of an "all clear signal"!

The craving for warm food was enough to motivate us to gather firewood and search for a place for a campfire. The dried wood and kindling quickly caught fire. We soon had sampurado (hot steamed rice flavored with chocolate, raw sugar and canned milk poured over it), helping to further calm our frayed nerves.

The men started building a lean-to made of cogon (thatched grass). My Mom and the women gathered dried grass, moss and soft leaves for the floor. We then laid blankets over them. My Mom was the only one who brought a mattress and we chose a corner for us.

While the adults were busy improvising a shelter, my friends and I began exploring around. As instructed, we stayed close together and remembered to move quietly. At first, the monotonous terrain didn't impress us. But as we went further down the slope, we heard the sound of rippling water. We eagerly ran towards the source. What we saw was enough to make us forget for a moment that we were refugees running for our lives. The river before our eyes was teeming with fish. We already had visions of learning how to set traps and having fresh fish for dinner every night. Much as we tried, we couldn't stifle cries of joy and ecstasy.

We continued downstream, carefully picking our way amongst the boulders and rocks along the bank of the river. Not faraway was a miniature cove where the water was shallow, sparkling clean and had the gentlest runoff. Around the edge of the shoreline of this cove was the thickest growth of foliage you ever saw. Again, screams of glee. We had discovered the perfect bathing area that afforded complete privacy! Our expressions of mirth and happiness were soon squelched. A parent heard us, came down to where we were and sternly scolded us for making so much commotion. Our frivolous expressions were short lived. Nevertheless, the feeling of contentment had settled. We had stumbled into our very own "paradise."

December and January was the best season to go into the Penaranda hills. The tropical heat wave was over and so are the monsoon rains. New growth begins and all life awaits the promise of sustenance. Fish are plentiful and birds have new songs to sing.

We asked ourselves, "Did we have a lesson to learn from them? We who had just gone through our own "fire of affliction" of fleeing from the enemy?""

Every person in our camp could identify with that. We too were survivors. How could we do less?

It was no accident that our first day in hiding happened to be on a Sunday. What a fitting tribute to Him… having a service amongst the trees.

The Sorianos were members of a Philippine Independent Methodist Evangelical Church and they too longed to give thanks to the Lord who protected and guided us to this haven.

> Faith of our father's living still,
> In spite of dungeon, fire and sword.
> Oh how our hearts leap high with joy.
> When're we hear that joyful word.
>
> Faith of our father's holy faith,
> We will be true to Thee till death!

We sang loud and true. Again, our parents reminded us with their scowls not to sing so loud. We couldn't help it; we were bursting in grateful melody. It seemed as if we were trying to compete with all the sounds of nature around us. We had arrived in a haven of refuge, a fortress.

At the end of the service, three smiling Filipino soldiers dressed in camouflaged fatigues came out of the bushes. Although they were obviously friendly and unarmed, most of us had to stifle a gasp of apprehension. Was the enemy lurking behind them?

They immediately noticed our shock at being discovered. In broken Tagalog, (they were natives of another region) they expressed the usual amenities and started telling us that they had been walking for miles around looking for direction. All they wanted to do was to hide out somewhere until it was safe enough for them to return to their families who lived in the Visayas, in a remote island south of Luzon where we lived. They were AWOL from the Philippine Army and did not want to be taken prisoners of war by the Japanese. They told us stories of how their platoon was ordered to retreat from the well-equipped and cruel Japanese Army.

Their stories of atrocities committed by the Japanese soldiers were so bizarre we found them hard to believe. We suspected their tales were exaggerated in order to get our sympathy. Little did we know that they were telling us the honest truth and how smart and lucky they were to have gone AWOL.

Understandably, they were anxious to get rid of their army clothes, so our men searched through their packs to see what clothes they could spare that would fit the three men. After burying their army fatigues, they confessed that they hid their rifles among the bushes where they were hiding. They wanted advice on what to do with them. Would the rifles come in handy in case the Japanese discovered us?

The women didn't want anything to do with such dangerous and implicating weapons. On the other hand, the Soriano men argued, the arms could be hidden in some unobtrusive place and only used during emergency. One of the soldiers suggested they could be used to hunt for food. Those two reasons were convincing enough to the womenfolk. The decision was made to keep the guns and ammunition.

The Filipino race as a whole is noted for their hospitality and natural inclination to include and or adopt anyone homeless and alone. So no one thought it unusual that the three just took it for granted that they could stay with us, eat and share what we had.

The folks decided that the disguise of the men was not convincing enough. Creative and further alterations had to be done. They thought of an added camouflage. Each of the men had to be adopted as one of our extended family. We gave each of them a different first name and baptized one as a Diaz and the other two as Sorianos. They were then "officially" part of our families.

Except for several friendly transients and passers by, who gave us welcome news about conditions in town, no one bothered us. Since we had no idea how long we would be in hiding, food was carefully rationed, but I can't recall a time when we went hungry.

My Mom's 100 lbs. sacks of rice lasted for the duration we were in hiding. With the men using discretion, the guns and ammunition proved to be indispensable. They purposefully went further into the hills, away from earshot of the Japanese and went searching for wild game. Occasionally, they would come home with wild chickens and geese. Once I remember feasting over a barbecued wild boar they had shot.

To pass the time, my Mom, who brought her sewing basket, stitched by hand outfits for my brother and I. We played "siklot", similar to jacks, using the smooth pebbles we found by the river. We dug holes by the riverbank to play sungka. Our favorite game was softball. We fashioned a ball out of a round rock the size of a golf ball wrapped thickly with several layers of old cotton socks. I remember the difficulty we had toning down our cheers when someone made a home run.

We were right in the middle of a softball game and my team was losing, when two men on horseback interrupted our game. I remember thinking to myself what a timely interruption it was, since I was getting frustrated watching our opponents make so many runs.

By this time, we were used to seeing travelers on foot. But seeing people on horseback was rare, especially with two horses in tow. Perhaps, I thought to myself, "they're only asking for directions." I did a double take. "Is that someone I know? It had been a year or so since I've seen them." My mind searched for a reason. Then I heard my brother calling me. He was screaming their names. "Ruthie, your Tata (uncles) Quiel and Carding. They're here!" How did my uncles find us? Their farm was scores of miles away. Was it by accident? There weren't even phone lines where we were. Nevertheless, here they were, bigger than life itself.

They had been on horseback for several days, stopping only to eat and rest briefly, questioning everyone they met if they had seen anyone with our description. They stopped at every camp, combing the whole countryside praying that they find us before any harm befell them or us.

My paternal grandparents wouldn't allow them to come home until they found us.

There was no time to loose. Packing only bare essentials, we left as quickly as they came. I had a crash course in riding a horse bareback.

We didn't have any knowledge of the whereabouts of the advancing Japanese army, so we evaded traveling near any highways. Without a compass, map nor written directions, my uncles amazingly found our way back to the safety of my paternal family's banana plantation. My grandparents were delirious with joy. They imagined the worst when my uncles hadn't returned at the allotted time. Like us, they had heard about the merciless Japanese Occupational Forces. My mother, brother and I were assigned to stay in my grandparents' home. But for the duration of our stay there, I spent most of my time next door.

Next door to my grandparents' house lived my youngest uncle, Tata Carding and his wife, Nana Nene. My grandparents had just played matchmaker for these two. Nana Nene was a widow of my older uncle, Tata Uro.

My grandparents were new converts of the Iglesia ni Cristo. Motivated by the zeal brought on by their new faith and its belief, they manipulated the two of them to get married.

Nana Nene was my idea of a model wife. The floors and windows of her nipa house were scrubbed clean with leaves of the "pang isis" tree until they were almost white. The yard was always swept and immaculate.

Unlike most of the wives in their village she was industrious and had foresight. With her carabao and little cart, she would go alone into the fields to gather firewood before the rains came.

She and her children were always clean, smelling of wild growing sweet herbs (reminiscent of commercially made camphor chests) she had gathered in the woods. She was careful not to uproot any of the plants when she picked them so that they would propagate themselves. After they were dried properly, she would tuck them under her trunk where she kept her clothes.

She had long, straight and black hair neatly knotted in a bun framed her delicate features. Nana Nene's skin was unusually fair and smooth which was the envy of most Filipino women. She was also unusually tall for a Filipina woman and with her regal bearing, she commanded attention wherever she went. I admit that I idolized my Nana Nene. At the market where she had a small stall, I would often visit her. There I learned about her being well known for her integrity and dependability. At the wholesalers, she was given priority, knowing that she could be trusted to pay her bills on time.

My grandparents shared the same fondness I had for Nana Nene. It didn't surprise me that they sought the church's counsel, used it to our advantage and kept her from remarrying outside of our family. Although no one ever heard her complain, Nana Nene's health deteriorated. Unable to work, she became impoverished and hospitalized. I saw her for the last time in one of the charity wards in a Manila hospital. She was only in her forties when she died. Part of me died as well.

My grandparent's banana plantation was called "Pula" (means red in Tagalog) and was reportedly bought with U.S. dollars my father sent home regularly. My grandfather labored long and hard to make it one of the largest banana plantations in that area.

Every summer after school, I could hardly wait to visit my grandparents. My Mom would dutifully deliver me at their house in Aduas and in their horse drawn caretela, we would make our arduous journey to Pula.

The roads were unpaved. During rainy season, mud was almost knee deep. I felt so sorry for the horse that pulled our caretela. Every so often, the wheels would get stuck in the muck.

My grandfather would alight from the vehicle and push one of the spokes of the wheel that was stuck while my grandmother and I prayed for strength for my grandfather and the horse. Often, passersby or residents of the sparsely populated village would volunteer to help, and then we could resume our journey only to be stuck again. I remember dreading those trips, holding my breath, dying a thousand deaths until we arrived at Pula.

These are a few of my paternal relations who made lasting impressions on me before the war. That was when community and family life was uninterrupted and unencumbered by ravages of war. I remember all of them with fondness.

My grandparents' farm Pula was considered almost a "promised land" because it produced many varieties of food. It had a small poultry, an orchard, piggery, milking carabaos, a granary that stored abundant supply of rice, rows and rows of vegetable plants. Its main crop was bananas.

In one corner of the plantation, my grandfather had donated a hectare of land to the government so that public education would be available to the residents of that sparsely populated area. A young female teacher was soon assigned to teach. When the war struck she went home to Manila, but came trudging back to Pula like a pied piper with her whole family consisting of her mother, grandmother, brother and his family, and an older spinster aunt.

Being true to the tradition of Filipino hospitality, my grandfather felt it was his obligation to house and feed these refugees too. With all those people requiring a constant supply of basic necessities, Pula's resources soon dwindled down, dangerous low. Sensing this, the schoolteacher's family soon left for their home in the capital city of Manila. Normalcy had not yet returned in town, so we decided to visit my Mom's second oldest sister, Ditche (Felisa Encarnacion Diaz).

We had been there for approximately a week, when my Mom suddenly contracted a high fever. The high temperature persisted for several days. Every adult suddenly became very solicitous of me. I sensed pity coming from them, anticipating the potential death of my Mom.

Ditche, second oldest sister of my mom, had a gift of healing, and tried every herb remedy and procedure she knew, but to no avail. So she sent for their oldest sister, Ating. She was the midwife, healer, and spiritual leader all rolled into one of the village of Aduas. She immediately came and with her herbs, prayers and procedures, including the use of her "laway" (saliva) she laid hands on my Mom.

The next day my mother's temperature subsided. After much discussion, her two sisters and brother-in-law decided that my Mom needed a more thorough exam by her own licensed physician. Even though normalcy had not returned in town, it was crucial for her health that they took the chance.

It took some ingenuity for my adult male cousins to devise a contraption to afford comfort for my Mom who was still weak from her bout with the fever. They decided a careton (carabao drawn cart) would be too bumpy a ride and might give my Mom a relapse of the dreaded fever. Dikong Canong, the strongest nephew, organized the team that took turns shouldering the two ends of a bamboo pole where a rattan hammock hung cradling my mom comfortably propped up on pillows.

On the way out of the farm, my Mom stopped them and told them she had to get "something" buried under a tree. They thought she was delirious and/or was hallucinating. She insisted that she couldn't leave the place unless she dug up what she had buried there. They finally had to give in and found to their surprise the jar filled with silver coins and jewelry.

When we got to the suburb of Cabanatuan, my ancestors' native village Aduas, we were relieved to find that a few of our relatives had already returned and were settling down to stay. On the way to Ating's house, we saw a sight that would remain forever in my memory. The Aduas Elementary School had been converted into a concentration camp for the survivors of the Bataan Death March. On April 10, 1942, the Bataan Death March began at dawn. The American and Philippine prisoners taken at Bataan were forced to march 85 miles in 6 days with but one meal of rice during the period. At the end of the march, which was punctuated with atrocities, more than 5,200 Americans and many more Filipinos had lost their lives.

At the school, we watched several American soldiers helping one extremely emaciated soldier to an outhouse. He relieved himself before they made it and the poor man was so sick to even be embarrassed. We thought about the three AWOL soldiers we adopted. We were so thankful they had deserted the army when they did, because of the deplorable physical condition of the prisoners of war and the cruel treatment they were receiving.

It wasn't very long before they dismantled the makeshift internment camp and moved the prisoners somewhere else. Our suspicions were that because the townspeople were sneaking food to the prisoners. At night they used sling shots to hurl hard-boiled eggs and fruit inside the compound.

To pass the time we learned to play Mahjong, a Chinese card game. Below us, on the make shift ground floor, our older brothers, uncles and their contemporaries played the game more seriously, with their betting and money transactions.

We sent word to Pilar, my Mom's cousin, who grew up with me and had evacuated to a neighboring village, Valde Puente, to come and join us.

Mahjong, village life and the added company of Pilar and Rosa were not stimulating enough for me, much less for my Mom. And because there was news from people who had been to town that the Japanese were leaving civilians alone, we thought it was high time for us to return and see for ourselves whether a rumor was true. Had our town been destroyed by fire?

With great trepidation, we approached the town, riding in a hired caretela. There were a few buildings left, but the closer we got to Sangitan, our part of town, the more we saw the ravages of a great fire that consumed houses. We could hardly recognize which block was ours. One great house was spared, it was located a block from where our boarding house had stood. A wrought iron fence surrounding a large yard with bushes and trees shielded it from being included in the inferno. Cinders and ashes were piled where the other wooden houses stood. The bigger the house, the higher were the piles of cinders and ashes. In between them, where the alleys divided the compounds of houses, ashes were noticeably lacking.

We had to use our memories to pinpoint exactly where our boarding house had stood. We remembered it had stood exactly in line across the street from the provincial capitol, so we had a point of reference.

Some of our neighbors were there too, shifting through the ashes, trying to salvage nails, and other metal objects such as hinges that could be used again to rebuild.

A few yards away, a group of people was listening intently to a news bearer. Excitedly, he reported seeing the Japanese Jujitsu instructor (our former neighbor) upon his arrival into town! He was dressed as an officer in the Imperial Army of Japan and was with other officers. The townspeople then started making conclusions that he was the one who ordered the razing of our neighborhood as a retaliation of the time when some youngsters mugged him. He had just been to a tavern and came home drunk. This happened only a few days before Pearl Harbor. It was a convincing hypothesis. Ours was the only neighborhood that had a great fire.

Amidst all the rubble and ashes, it was almost impossible to find the lot where our boarding house had stood. But we kept looking.

Almost simultaneously, my friends and I gasped with recognition. There it was, the concrete porch we desperately wanted to find. It looked like a small mountain of ashes and cinders. Ours was the only building in the neighborhood that had that size and shape of a porch. My companions and I quickly ran towards it. With our bare hands, it took us only a few minutes to brush off the ashes from the opening. It was large enough, so the three of us poked our heads in. Our blinded eyes brought on by the brilliant noon sun outside took time to adjust to the dark interior of the porch. But as soon as our eyes got adjusted we saw and confirmed what we had been praying to be true. Our valuables were intact, all of them obviously untouched, completely saved from the fire and looters.

So sudden was our mourning turned into rejoicing. It was incredible, finding them all in such good condition. These were our heirlooms linked to our past giving us our sense of identity... ultimately security.

Reverently, one by one we took out the boxes and crates. My Mom could not contain her amazement at how well they still looked. Only edges of some papers had slight traces of brown caused by the intense heat of the fire. The thick, almost one-foot walls of concrete were able to safely block out what must have been an inferno.

The driver of our caretela helped us load our cargo that we felt was even more precious now. We brought them all home to where we were temporarily staying. Later, my Mom had to store them with different relatives who had the proper storage in their homes. Our set of dishes, silver and glassware went to a niece, Ditcheng Canding. Our trunk of miscellaneous things went to Lola Ninay's where, after my Mom did some remodeling, we were later invited to live.

Soon my Mom experienced perhaps the greatest loss she had during the war and it took her several years to get over it. The jar of heirloom jewels she carried with her all throughout the evacuation, and kept safe from looters and thieves. One evening, after supper, she was down in the ground floor of Lola Ninay's house talking with her nephews and nieces who had just arrived from Aduas. There was some unrest in their village, so they were spending the night with us. She had her jewels carefully bundled up in a large handkerchief with its corners tightly knotted together to prevent them from spilling out. It was customary for older women at the time to place valuables underneath their clothing in their chests, between the breasts. It was an unusually warm evening and she was perspiring profusely, so she took out the bundle from her chest to air it out. She placed the bundle down beside her. That was her last recollection of the precious jewels. She thought she had forgotten to pick it up and had accidentally left it on the bench beside her.

That night, while undressing for bed, she realized it was gone. She quickly called every person staying with us, including an elderly couple that was renting one of the rooms in the ground floor. Nobody would admit to having seen the jewels. She approached the Mayor of our town who was a distant relative, thinking he could help investigate the matter. He immediately imprisoned and interrogated the renter who vehemently denied seeing the jewels, much less taking them. My Mom's hair turned gray almost overnight and she lost her appetite and weight. Sleep no longer came easy for her and she never learned what happened to them.

By that time, my brother had moved back to Manila and had a "buy and sell" business in Manila. He was doing well. He was staying in one of the finest hotels there, hobnobbed with "high society" and learned to indulge in their gambling game of Jai alai! He was oozing with Japanese currency, which he carried in "bayongs" (large bags made out of cocoanut leaves). He owned a horse drawn "calesa" and a racehorse that gave him status.

Like a dutiful son, he invited us to move to Manila. He would take care of our rental payments. He also suggested that I go to school. We packed what few belongings we had and took the train for the city of Manila.

Ating, my Mom's oldest sister had a daughter in the district of Paco. Although her husband's house was small and was already crowded with her in-laws and two small children, she invited us to stay with her and was willing to put us up until we found an apartment of our own.

Meanwhile, my brother enrolled me at the Marina Institute, a secretarial vocational school. It was a project of the University of the Philippines Alumni Association, which tried to maintain the high standards that the University was known for.

Returning to school after three years was a welcome stimulus I needed. Our required subjects were well balanced, and also included folk dancing, which was part of our Physical Education program. Learning and writing the Japanese language was mandatory. Performing our dances for the Japanese officials was one of the purposes of our long hours of rehearsals. We quickly learned disgust for our conquerors.

It was in the Paco neighborhood that I met Melecio Vega, Jr. He was the only child of Francisca Morales Vega. My Mom and Mrs. Vega were past acquaintances. As one of the home economics supervisors of the School of Education, she had boarded with us in Cabanatuan during her annual inspection visits to our town. I remember Mrs. Vega as one of the most reserved women I had ever met and she had the proverbial "poker face."

Mel and the other teenagers of the neighborhood had a social club. It was called "Buklod na Guinto" (chain of gold). It didn't take them long to invite me to join them, elected me as vice-president and become a part of the neighborhood.

After several months, my Mom was able to find an apartment for her and me in Santa Ana, not too far from the city center. It was a triplex and only a studio, but had an added loft for a bedroom. A high wall of concrete fenced in the backyard for privacy. It seemed ample enough for my Mom and me.

We finally had our very own place. We felt secure there amongst friends; my aunt and church members living close by. The only disadvantage was that it took twenty minutes to commute to school on a crowded trolley.

Immediately, we got involved at church. I joined the church choir and helped in the Sunday School program. For the first time since the Japanese Occupation, we felt normalcy had returned. Humble as it was, we enjoyed the privacy of having our own place.

Living in the suburbs of Manila seemed relatively peaceful enough until one late afternoon. My friend, the only son of the Buados, had just taken me home from a date to the movies. The following morning, I received word that he was nowhere to be found. I was the last person known to have been with him and seen him. We became frantic. The whole church formed search parties, interrogating people and combing the town.

Finally, after a couple of days, he was found badly wounded in a ravine in the outskirts of town. He was semi-conscious and barely remembered that a Japanese sentry had suspected him of something he couldn't even remember. He was bayoneted by the same sentry in the back, dumped and left for dead in the ravine. It took him months to recover.

In a year, I graduated from the University of the Philippines Marina Institute and was immediately hired as secretary to Rev. Benjamin Guansing, the first Filipino minister of Central Church in Manila.

One day, the Americans started bombing the city. In the beginning we silently cheered when we heard their bombs drop. No one bothered to man the air raid signal stations since the Japanese themselves were on the verge of panic.

Next door to the parsonage where I had my office was the church building. Unbeknownst to me at the time was a group of church young people, including a cousin of mine who secretly listened regularly to an illegal shortwave set under the choir loft which the Japanese banned. The Japanese were on a campaign for a "Greater East Asia Co-Prosperity Sphere" and censored all news that didn't serve their purposes. They were heavily involved in propaganda tactics.

One of their "headlines" read: Japanese Imperial Forces land on American soil, Japan on the verge of winning the war!" Through the church basement grapevine, we found out that they had a short-lived foot hold on the uninhabited island of Attu in the Aleutian Islands of Alaska!

These people who risked their lives listening to short wave radio had actually heard that the Americans had landed in Leyte! It was incredible news and seemed too good to be true.

But tragedy struck, and the group was caught red handed. Dever Alejandro, my cousin, and others were imprisoned and subsequently shot to death!

I was in the middle of typing a letter when bombings became more frequent. Pastor Guansing, my boss, announced that they were going to evacuate and that I should go home. I hurriedly packed my few belongings, took a jeep and left.

My Mom was not home; only "Puppy" our grown dog was there to greet me. The neighbors told me that she had gone to Novaliches to buy rice. She did not expect my coming home.

I remember an older lady, a member of our congregation, living alone two or three houses from us. She had been sick for several days in her one room shack. It was my privilege to visit her everyday and share some of our hoarded rice, which I would cook for her. She had no other food in the house except what I brought her.

Inflation rose to astronomical heights. Many people could not afford to buy food. Looting and stealing became rampant. In order to stretch their dwindling supply of rice, our neighbors and most of the population who didn't have the foresight to stock up on food, as my mom had, resorted to eating "lugaw" (rice gruel) instead of the usual steamed rice. Other staples also became more scarce and difficult to afford. Some streets were lined with beggars. It was not uncommon to see a mother with two or more malnourished toddlers and an emaciated infant in her arms begging for food. Garbage heaps were frequented by hordes of scavenging humans.

My mom's God-given foresight served us well and had anyone known we had a large hoard of rice, our lives would have been in jeopardy. Even my closest friends who came often to visit never had any idea that we had a gold mine in our bedroom. No one suspected that the "studio couch" that had a firm mattress and a nondescript bedspread concealed six 100 lbs sacks of rice. My Mom had them all lined up against the wall placed a piece of plywood over them, then laid a mattress and covered them with a bedspread that trailed to the floor.

None of our friends and acquaintances actually starved to death, but some of them were very close to it. Very often I would sneak out a few cups out of this abundant supply and share it with some of my closest friends who sometimes were too embarrassed to accept. No one was known to still have any extra food to share. They assumed we were sharing ours at an extreme sacrifice. Except for the very rich, we were the only ones left eating balanced meals. Once again, my Mom's gift of foresight came to the fore.

Even before there was any sign of an impending food shortage, my Mom, with her green thumb, decided to convert an 8'x3' parking strip in front of our apartment into a sweet potato patch. The soil was too rocky to produce any potatoes, but the shoots made the best salad and greens to mix in with soup. Our cemented patio in the back became a "poultry" consisting of a couple of hens that faithfully laid an egg each day. We rationed our stock of canned foods leftovers from our dormitory supply.

One afternoon as I was unpacking, having just arrived from my job at the Guansings, we heard anti-aircraft explosions. Sta. Ana didn't have a community bomb shelter, so I just crouched behind a three-foot concrete wall in our living room. Outside, neighbors were milling around. No one showed fear of being hit by shrapnel or stray bullets! I soon discovered why. Above them flew a squadron of B-29's marked U.S.A. They were confident that the U.S. planes wouldn't drop bombs on civilians since we were their allies.

With their faces uplifted, one hand shielding their eyes from the bright noonday sun, the other waving wildly, they were jumping up and down cheering loudly. They were exuberant over our liberators coming to end four years of oppressive occupation by the Japanese. At last we had evidence that the U.S. and perhaps even

MacArthur had actually returned. People were in a state of celebration and I went outdoors and joined them. Our joy couldn't be contained!

It was surreal. All around the planes were explosive anti-aircraft shelling, resembling Fourth of July firecrackers. We wondered about their precise formation, seemingly ignoring the danger of getting hit. In less than a second, before we could blink an eye, one of the B-29's left its formation and came spiraling down, leaving a trail of black smoke. We watched in total unbelief. It wasn't what we expected at all. Then out of the burning plane four parachutes unfolded and slowly began to descend. Then came the sound of automatic rifles which seemed to be just a block away.

Still reeling from what we had just seen, the crowd dispersed. I went home, looked for my dog and had him take care of the throbbing sore on my ankle. (I had developed a festering sore on my right ankle. Faith healers in the Philippines believed that dogs could heal wounds by licking them). Since I was all out of medication and in intense pain, I resorted to this ancient practice. I had Puppy lick my wound. It didn't ease the pain, but the wound looked clean. The abortive celebration left me exhausted so I sought the relief of sleep.

I woke up to heavy, urgent pounding on my door. It was my friend and neighbor, Rodrigo Estrada. He had been running and was breathlessly relating to me about the parachutist who landed behind our houses, in practically our backyard! Throwing all caution to the wind, I dashed out of the house, forgetting the pain in my ankle.

There was the parachutist in the middle of a gaping crowd, immobilized. His boyish freckled face and red kinky hair in sharp contrast to the brown faces and black haired crowd surrounding him. His eyes were shut. He appeared to be asleep. No one had the courage to touch him. Everyone had anguish written on their faces. Intermittently someone in the crowd would whisper. "What can we do? If the Japanese found him, he'd really be tortured!" Someone suggested we hide him somewhere. Where would we hide him? Nobody knew what to do, so no one did anything.

Someone finally got the courage to take his pulse and after what seemed an eternity, he shook his head and said, "It's no use, he is already dead."

An agonizing groan rose from the crowd. Hushed comments of: "Sayang na sayang." (What a pity, a terrible pity!) Our hopes for instant liberation were dashed to pieces. Slowly, the crowd dispersed, some shaking their heads in unbelief, some in shock.

I thought about his family in the States. I bent down so I could read his name and address from his dog tag. Someone yelled, "Don't do it, the Japanese are coming to investigate. You'll be suspected of collaborating with their enemy." He had barely finished what he was saying when two Japanese sentries we recognized came and dragged the parachutist away. I got up, went home, and cried.

Nightfall came. I looked forward to the comfort and escape of sleep. As I was preparing for bed, tying the stringed corners of my mosquito netting, I heard commotion outside my bedroom window. The neighbors were out gazing unbelievingly towards the city. On the horizon we saw what appeared to be an inferno right in the middle of Manila.

I went inside our apartment wondering what was going to happen next. As the night wore on, outside my window, the pavement echoed the tramping of boots. I froze in fear. They had to be Japanese soldiers either escaping the fire or retreating. There were many of them, like several platoons.

On the ground floor next to where my bed was located was a hole large enough for a person to crawl through. A large piece of shrapnel from some kind of ammunition landed there earlier that day. I fought the urge to panic. I began planning for an escape route in case some soldiers saw the gaping hole and found me inside. At the rear of our apartment was the patio enclosed by a concrete wall too high for me to scale. On the other side of us was an adjacent apartment. All the windows were barred. An escape route was impossible and I was trapped.

Puppy must have instinctively felt my whole being throbbing with adrenaline. He jumped up on my bed, cuddled close to me and tried to reassure me with his whimpering. I cupped his snout. He obeyed and kept quiet.

The sound of retreating soldiers kept on and intense fear continued to grip me. I felt for my Bible next to me. I wanted reassuring words of comfort. But how was I to read in the dark? Beside me was some dark sheeting we used for "blackouts" on the windows. I laid the sheeting on top of the netting and allowed the sides to cover it. I had a perfect "blackout." I then groped for a match and lit a candle. With one flip of the pages of the Bible I was led to the familiar words I needed for comfort, Psalm 91

> He that dwelleth in the secret place of the Most High
> shall abide under the shadow of the Almighty.
> I will say of the Lord, He is my refuge and my fortress:
> my God; in Him will I trust.
>
> Thou shalt not be afraid for the terror by night;
> nor for the arrow that flieth by day;
> Nor for the pestilence that walketh in darkness;
> nor for the destruction that wasteth at noonday.
>
> A thousand shall fall at thy side,
> and ten thousand at thy right hand;
> but it shall not come nigh thee.
>
> There shall no evil befall thee,
> neither shall any plague come nigh thy dwelling.
>
> For he shall give his angels charge over thee,
> to keep thee in all thy ways.

Slowly the intensity of my fears subsided. The echoing "tramp, tramp" of boots on the pavement subsided. Puppy and I survived the night.

The next day I was told that Hans Arber, a Swiss national, had converted the nearby elementary school into a refugee center. He was interviewing for a secretary. My short secretarial experience with Rev. Guansing proved valuable; I was hired on the spot and started typing the census.

Scores of homeless and injured people had to be housed, fed and treated. They had fled from the city to escape the fires ignited by the retreating Japanese soldiers. As they were fleeing, some were massacred and shot by these same soldiers. Others escaped unharmed, but some came to the center badly wounded.

Business was at a standstill. Food was nowhere to be found, much less bought. The economy was in a state of confusion. Japanese currency was worthless and anyone who still possessed Philippine peses was reluctant to spend the "peacetime" stable currency.

Immediately, American troops began showing up with truckloads of rice, cases of sardines and medical supplies. PCAU (The Philippine Civilian Assistance Unit), an emergency corps, organized by the U.S. Army became the lifeblood of Manila.

We, the employees of the Refugee Center, got paid in gantas of rice and cans of sardines. For at least a month, rice and sardines became our daily fare. When we were hot, even our perspiration smelled of sardines.

One sunny afternoon, with my Mom's permission, we decided to check out a G.I. camp in the outskirts of town. My Mom who associated Americans with her exclusive experience limited to only missionaries was naive enough to allow me and another young girlfriend to visit this camp.

We arrived in the tent city. We were the only women except for one or two who were heavily made up and wore seductive clothes. These women didn't even give us a clue to what we were about to experience.

Two G.I.s approached us with whiskey bottles in their hands smiling broadly. I, who was more proficient in English, introduced us. Lolly Castro, my friend who was more physically endowed than I was, was picked first. The other G.I. sized me up with his friendly stare. Naively, I thought him very friendly and sincere. The two of them invited us to sit underneath a tree by a little pond away from the rest of the tent city. We followed obligingly hoping they would offer us some of the bacon being fried nearby.

We were getting awfully tired of sardines.

I was intent on getting to know these two guys. I began my barrage of questions wondering at the same time why they were insisting we join them in their drinks after we told them that we don't touch the stuff. The two G.I.s finally sensed that we were not the type of girls they mistook us to be and sent us away with a slab of bacon each.

The next day seemingly started uneventful. I was seated at my typewriter typing a letter dictated an hour ago by my boss, Hans

Arber, when along came Mrs. Asuncion Perez, the Director of Public Welfare and Services doing her round of finding Refugee homes. She happened to be a family friend of ours and had known me as a child. After the usual amenities, she immediately asked me, "Do you know that American citizens are being offered repatriation back to the United States?" She said further that her son, also born in the U.S. had already been approved for repatriation and was en route. She gave me the address of where to apply.

I brought my Dad's last letter with me. The Red Cross tried to find him at his last address, but it took several days before they found he had moved. His cablegram read: "Come home, anxious to see you." More red tape ensued. The CIA investigated my past for subversive activities. Physical examinations and inoculations took weeks to accomplish. I resigned from my duties at the Refugee Center and resided close to the processing center at the University of Santo Tomas where only a couple of months ago American prisoners of war were confined and tortured.

On June 13, 1945, I and about twenty or so American dependents sailed for America on the troop ship U.S.S. Gen. Harry Taylor. Japan and the U.S. would not sign a peace treaty for another three months. On land, the Japanese kept fighting and were reluctant to surrender. The Pacific Ocean was still dotted with mines and a few Japanese submarines were lurking in the deep with their ever-ready torpedoes. On board the ship, battle weary and injured G.I.s were part of the panorama. Stateroom beds were reserved only for the captain and his mate, so we were allotted barrack type bunk beds to sleep on. Food was the unfamiliar and typical Navy grub. It was a far cry from being a luxury liner, but we boarded the ship and left Manila harbor in a state of euphoria.

As soon as we were settled in our assigned spaces, air raid, and evacuation drills began. Amidst the friendly stares, wolf whistles and smiles of the troops, we were given a tour of the different areas of the ship. The most frequented post was the PX where we went wild spending the $35.00 the Red Cross had given each of us to spend for toiletries and other needs.

An entry in my diary, around that time, reveals my heart's desire for mercy and strength. I wrote:

May 10, 1945...

Again these pages lifts the heavy mists of the unforgettable past. Today as I remember once more the thrilling episode of that once upon a time regime, it gives me a queer feeling; a sort of mystery that enables me to think of my non-existence. Incredible. That is the word. Unbelievable that in spite of people, me being first, uselessness unworthiness, lack of trust and faith in him, He until now has been giving us that one supreme necessity all of us cling to: **God grant us the power to live.**

Although I did not know it at the time, what lay ahead was college in the northwestern corner of America. It was going to be the start of a whole new chapter in my life.

TWO

RUTH'S ARRIVAL IN AMERICA

"Great is thy faithfulness, morning by
morning new mercies we see.
All we have needed thy hand has provided.
Great is thy faithfulness!" Amen
Hymn

Arriving in San Francisco, the American Red Cross contacted my father whom I had not seen in many years. Once at my father's house, it didn't take but three days to realize my father's ways had not changed. The married woman across the street had several children, and my dad fathered two of them.

While I was dealing with the realities of his life, the Lord began to present opportunities for me to speak about the war at numerous church functions. The first time, I lost myself in tears, unable to speak. Eventually I was able to be more composed. Even now, more than fifty years later, there are times when those memories bring the suffering, pain and loss freshly to the surface.

Yet again, the mystery of the Lord was present in preparing me to bring use to those memories. Instead of erasing them, the Lord empowered me to speak not only of what happened but how I recovered and carried my life forward. God had indeed granted me the *"power to live!"*

Realizing there was no future for me in California, I returned to my mother's roots in the Northwest and enrolled in college. While there, my diary concludes of the war…

April 15, 1948

"What words can describe thy unsurpassable power and might? Looking back to the hardships and tribulations we've passed, one cannot believe that people like us would be given another chance, again, to live. And in living this life, one may have this thing readily in mind; that this chance is being given to us for a better and much holier tomorrow. Not that lowering of our status, but something purer, nobler, and more sublime would be added in lives that once were nearly lost and now are gathered up from ruin."

The war was over. In America, free to pursue who I was in Christ, I encountered a different battle: racism.

Popular with my friends and carefree as ever, I embraced college life with my childhood gusto. All that came to a halt when the Dean of the college called me into her office and announced I was not to date white boys anymore. It could end in marriage and they didn't want any more 'half breeds.'

Death could not have felt worse. The Caucasian young man I was dating at the time asked me to marry him just to make a statement against the Dean's position. Wisely, I declined his offer, knowing it wasn't right.

The next years were miserable for me. Outwardly, I stayed involved and active in church experiences, organizing many educational and recreational activities for Filipino Christian youth in the area. Inwardly, I simply passed them.

During harsh times, God always presents interesting moments to alert us to His presence and loving care when we suffer persecution. So it was that, on one particular day during a time at a church camp near the college, I was introduced to a woman who had driven to the campus specifically to meet me. Face to face at last, I could meet my namesake: Ruth Fogle, the head of the Deaconess Training School that my mother attended before my birth. She had heard of my enthusiasm for ministry and wanted to meet me in person. What a tremendous reminder from the Lord that my rich spiritual heritage was a personal gift. I was and had always been in His positive regard, no matter what others said or did.

Senior year there were some friends who decided to cheer me up by entering me in the homecoming Queen contest. My roommate was one of the vote counters and she felt it was her duty to let me know I had lost by only a few votes. It didn't matter to me. I was in the court and had the good wishes of my friends. Years later, I ran into someone who, not knowing who I was, reflected back on that time. When I told her who I was, her face paled. Come to find out, I had actually won the contest and the vote had been adjusted so a white girl would win instead.

It was not yet time by God's clock to heal me of mounting incidences of prejudice.

Graduate studies in Social Work followed graduating from college. There I met a handsome young man with dreams of finding success in fisheries. After many years of ardently pursuing higher ground, I had a moment of weakness when my family pressured me into the marriage. Not knowing, or able, to stand up for my own feelings, I married a fellow Filipino.

The dreams and visions of success fell flat. In an attempt to support his efforts, I agreed to move back to the Philippines so we could be close to his mother, along with our first child in tow. Although my mother-in-law exhibited cultural ways that she loved me, seven years of deprivation followed. Poor beyond measure, there were multiple miscarriages and three more live births; my second son and two daughters. Living off my mother in law was almost more than I could bear. On one occasion, I was leading my children in grace before a meal. After the prayer, my mother in law remarked, "Why are you thanking God when *I'm* the one that's providing!"

I was still committed to morally supporting and staying with my husband in his dream of owning a fish farm. I agreed to move with him to a remote and undeveloped area. My oldest son refers to it as the "time we lived in the jungle." The only clean drinking water was available by collecting rainwater. The business was a disaster. Later, he briefly took a job teaching at a government sponsored school of fisheries during which time we continued to live a primitive life style with no electricity, running water, and extremely unsanitary conditions.

I finally reached a breaking point. I demanded from God an explanation of his earlier promise to me through Philippians 2:10: "Every knee shall bow...." I cried bitterly and was lead to read Philippians 4:19, "But my God shall supply all your need according to his riches in glory by Christ Jesus." With God's word in my heart, I decided then and there to come back to America. My decision became almost an obsession. I no longer felt trapped. The Lord had given me a ray of Hope. In spite of our poverty, I had the assurance of provision for all our needs. Scraping together my resources, I took my four children home to the States. I prayed my husband would follow.

My husband did follow us to the States but things didn't improve, in fact, it got much worse. He started one business after another all ending up debt ridden. With unwavering faith, I went to my pastor. Laying out the whole story, I trusted in his wisdom when he said he felt I needed to see a lawyer who could help. The lawyer explained that I had no choice but to divorce because legally I was also responsible for all of his debts.

Good Methodist that I was, I did not drink alcohol. When I met my husband my opinion changed. He drank and I would join him. Now in the States, realizing I was in a seemingly hopeless mess, caught in the blues that can overtake even the most faithful of Christians, I saw a half full open bottle of Champagne on the table. Wishing only to make the pain of it all go away, I drank it all. Far from relieving the pain, I was sick to my stomach and woke up the next morning feeling worse than ever. I lay on my bed distraught, bedraggled, hopeless, feeling as if I was a total failure. I wanted to cry out to the Lord from the depths of my soul. To my amazement, no words came out, but I heard myself babbling unintelligently. Immediately, I felt relief and I couldn't understand why. Looking back after reading "Nine O'clock in the Morning" by Father Bennett of Ballard St. Luke's Church, I realized the Lord had gifted me with what the charismatic movement starting at that time called "a baptism of the Holy Spirit."

What a teachable moment of awe for God's higher ways! A dam of hope broke loose! My spiritual life seemingly like a film on slow motion started to gain momentum and began to accelerate.

I look back on my life and know I would be living in the gutter if it were not for the Grace of God. Truth is reality and truth makes us really appreciate the Lord and what He's done. He's the same yesterday and today. If he's seen us through and protected us in that past, he's not going to stop now. He never changes.

After twenty-two years of married life, I divorced my husband, not joyfully or willingly, but obediently. God gave me the determination. Sometimes, God can grant a determination that's so strong it's frightening. It has kept me out of a lot of danger.

For years, every time I heard a popular song (of that era), "You Never Belong to Me, but I Can Dream, Can't I?" It was one of my ex-husband's favorite songs, and it baffled and saddened me. After our divorce, I would weep at the loss of the relationship. One time of weeping, the Lord interrupted my tears and said, "That's right, you never belonged to him and NEVER will you! You have always belonged to me." I was ironing in the basement of my roommate friend's house that had about ten or more steps. I flew up on 'wings' and hardly felt my feet touching the stairs to relate to her what had just happened. The resonance of the hymn of my childhood came into being: "Now I belong to Jesus. Jesus belongs to me. Not for the years of time alone, but for eternity." To this day, I pray, by His grace that the song resonates again at a time when I will need it, using it as one of my armors against the wiles of the enemy.

Many other healing encounters took place over the following week. I realized God had been there every step of the way. I was reminded again that I belonged to God even before I was born. It is the life giving realization.

During this time period, there was another life-changing situation that God revealed his great love and provision for me; a love and provision He has for all of us.

I have always been a fitness buff. Hiking, sports, walking, jumping on a small trampoline, and swimming have all been a part of my regular routine. Right after the divorce was completed, I was doing my lap swim and I slammed my head into the edge of the pool. Although I immediately saw a blinding white light, I was not alarmed. I completed my swim and went home. The next day, the lump on my head was so large; another teacher at the school where I taught insisted I go to see the doctor. I fell asleep in the waiting room and was not able to count backwards as instructed by the doctor. I laughed the symptoms off as fatigue and a poor aptitude with numbers. The doctor told me I should probably stay home from school a day and rest.

Rest does not come easily because of my perpetual motion. A free day at home, I set about washing my windows. By noon I was tired and laid down for a short rest. When I tried to get up, I was completely paralyzed. All I could move were my eyes and my mouth. I called to my daughter in law who was staying with me at the time. An ambulance arrived and off I went to the hospital.

Weeks earlier, a guy one of my daughters was dating, Koji, showed me a picture of his mother. I instantly recognized her and recalled her name. She was a Japanese woman, fairly new to the U.S., who worked in records at Harborview Hospital where I was working as a social worker. In God's infinite ways, Koji gave her the shocking news that I was admitted to Swedish Hospital with full-blown paralysis and none of the numerous tests revealed the cause of it.

Koji's mom slipped up to my room after her shift and after visiting hours. In spite of the excitement of seeing her again, she was able to get me to relax in the midst of my traumatic divorce. We laughed freely as we recalled old times. God sent me a wonderful gift of healing by providing someone to care for me that I hadn't seen in years.

Before the evening was through, I found my shoulders were able to move after laughing so hard, and my arms began to come alive.

Apparently what had happened was a slow swelling of the brain as a result of the blow against the pool. I was in the hospital for a month. Slowly the paralysis healed. People from church came and prayed with me. One of my daughters read the Bible to me. Friends returned many times. At last, I was able to move enough to go home. God's provision again sent the right person at the right time. Another friend who was also divorced came from Alaska to care for me until I was fully recovered.

It was tangible evidence that no matter what happened to me, the Lord was going to supply all I needed.

We have such a rich God. He is the source of all we need. How does he do it? He is Love and we are created in His image. We belong to Him and He belongs to us! Some of our needs are met immediately. Some needs take longer to be met. Some are met in tangible ways. He always meets our need in His time. It is the Faith that He authors which makes it possible for us to see and experience that his promise is true. He supplies every need we have whether it is for protection, physical healing, healing of memories, restoration in a relationship, or more time. Whatever we need, he provides people and orchestrates circumstances in manners that are above our ways and thoughts. We need to go to God to have the scales of our eyes removed and have Him open our ears. When we don't get what we ask for, it is perhaps not in His plan for us. Some things we think we need are really just wants. It is wonderful when what we want is an alignment with His plan. This is possible and it is a gift. Other times, He has creative ways we cannot understand but we can trust in his sovereignty. Occasionally people learn this early in their Christian journey. For others, it takes time and includes having these truths tested through the crucible of affliction and tribulation.

Now that I was healed, it was time for me to move on.

Initially after my divorce, I honestly hated men. So, of course God led someone to invite me to a Christian singles group. God does not allow hate to stand stagnant in our hearts. I went kicking and screaming and my friends prayed for me.

The dates with the men that followed were so abundant that, at my house, one was coming in the front door while another was going out the back door. Far from out of control social behavior, it was God's way of healing me from hatred. I discovered there were many nice men in the world.

The singles group was an interdenominational bunch that met at a restaurant. Having been started by a recently widowed school principal, it was a well-organized fellowship with Bible Study and recreational activities and support networks covering every possible interest.

A young man named Tom joined for the sports activities. He had recently moved from the East Coast and another of the men in the group felt the need to pray earnestly for Tom to accept Jesus Christ as his Lord and Savior. Little did we realize that the Lord was about to bring our lives closer together than either of us ever imagined two lives could be, in service to the Lord.

THREE

TOM GRIME

What is it like to tell the story of my childhood when I mostly can't remember? A struggle.

I am a person who was, before the Lord healed me, completely shut down by childhood trauma. Sometimes I do happen upon a truth from that time in my life. Once revealed, that truth can be repeated like a favorite story.

I came from a rigid New England family. My mother was an impeccable housekeeper. My father was a man who liked order in all things. They were a perfect pair, in their woundedness.

Our family lived a life so well contained, within the walls of our house; birthdays were rarely celebrated with parties. People never visited our home. Visits were so infrequent that if someone did come, I hid under my bed.

The call on my life was as clear as the call on Ruth's, though our paths were one hundred eighty degrees different. Perhaps those of us in the church would like to think of the call to ministry as coming from roots of evangelical passion, or perhaps a tawdry past with a holy repentance that leaves beer bottles and cigarette butts in its wake. But what about the truly transforming conversion? What of a conversion like mine that is so deep that the mind and the emotions follow the yielding of the Spirit?

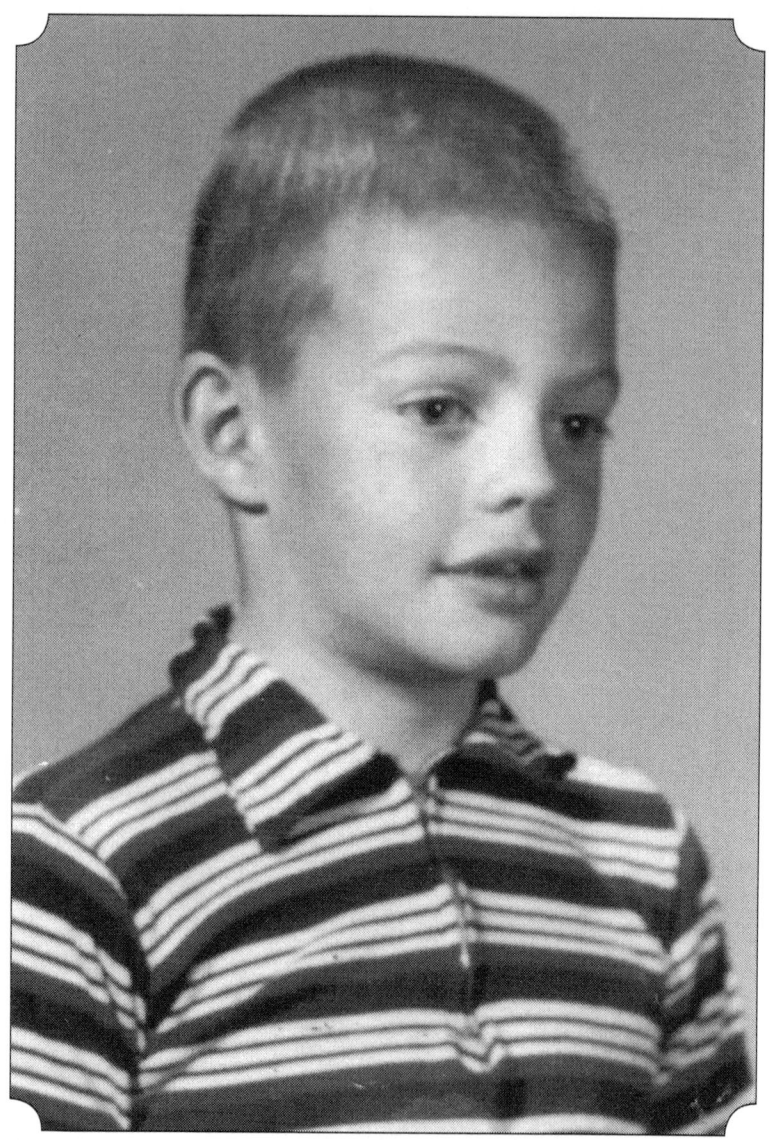

Tom Grime at eight-years old.

The physical details are a good place to start to tell the story. The town, in which, our family lived was the quintessential, beautiful, New England town. The only notable characteristic was a woman's college located there. The college and its influence on the town were quite substantial. Academically, it attracted a certain kind of person and financially, it brought in a lot of private money.

The house we lived in was new. It was an ambitious financial step for my parents; and their pride was evident everyday.

My own bedroom was on the main floor next to my parents. Two windows looked out on the back yard and I could look out and see the birds. My mother took a special interest in the birds. In winter, she would put out seeds and suet so they would come where she could see them.

There was a fast growing willow tree in the back yard because a hill behind the house created a bog like condition with run off water settling in the flat spots. In reflection, I suppose, my bedroom was the best room in the house.

The floors were oak hardwood that had to be polished. I had to watch for splinters. There was a rectangular carpet beside my bed with a Native American design on it. Of course, I don't know where it came from. Maybe my grandmother, because it looked like something she would have chosen for my room. It was too radical a design for my parents.

The other special item in my room was a piano. My dad liked to play it in the evening and it had a calming effect on him. I think it was one of the few times my dad actually enjoyed himself because he was happy with the music. Sometimes he would smoke his pipe while he played. I don't remember this for sure, but I think my dad could play and sing well also. My parents never asked if I would like to learn to play. I remember hearing my grandfather play the piano as well. My dad's two sisters both had beautiful voices and sang in their church. Later in life, I tried playing the piano. I was slow to learn but I sure loved its tone. As far as I know, neither of my sisters wanted or ever mentioned the piano.

I always feel a bit disjointed trying to tell about my childhood. The cohesiveness comes in the effort to put together the 'why' of the picture. My journey has been trying to put my internal and external life into the same sphere. Locking them in step with each other has provided a challenge for someone like me. Although blessed with all the social graces of a perfectly brought up New Englander, on closer examination, the effort to integrate thought, feeling, and action results in emotional lurchings. Remember always, such healing is not beyond the realm of possibility for someone who is willing to be healed. I have been willing to be healed of love wounds so deep only the Lord could touch them.

I also don't know why but my room was always neat. Wouldn't that be the kind of thing a person would remember as they recalled who they were as a child? Do you understand the depths to which I cannot do that? Well defended from the emotional austerity and rage that was the dynamic of my parent's household; do not underestimate how severely I am disconnected from my childhood. Locked away in the folds of memory, I have recently taken steps to bring those memories into the light. Still, I don't know why the room was always neat.

My mother's fastidiousness, no doubt, had something to do with it. She had been a nurse during World War II, stationed in a MASH unit in France, treating young men for burns received in fighting. It must have been horrible for her: a small town girl thrust into a hell of blood, screams and helplessness. I think she was scarred for life.

I remember she made the sheets on my bed so tight; I could never get into or under them. She would square off the corners with not a wrinkle to be found. I would first always pull off the sheets because I needed extra room for my feet and toes because I was so tall. I hated the feeling of the clean sheets. I much preferred the wrinkled up old sheets. After all that work I would come along and wreck it.

I have two sisters; a twin to whom I have never been close to, and an older sister who was cut off emotionally from the family at the age of one. With a limited emotional repertoire, the twins who followed only a year after my oldest sister's birth overwhelmed my parents. There was not enough love or attention to give to Connie. She was on her own.

I do remember my sisters were sometimes mad at me because my room was always so neat. They lived upstairs in a big room. I remember thinking it was so far away...all the way up those long stairs. My grandmother would sometimes stay in a room up there too. They also didn't like it that I was saving my money. Because it was the 1950's, I had more options as a male to earn money and I opened up a savings account. I still have the passbook.

My father was a supervisor in a textile plant. In the course of its manufacturing, the factory had some major problems with production. My dad redesigned the looms and fixed them in a certain way to keep them going. His accomplishments did not go by unnoticed and he was richly compensated.

Our family lived our days in tandem. Meeting our obligations with flawless routine, my father and mother controlled things in their own unique ways; my father with anger, my mother with more passive aggressive manipulation.

They were married for forty years when she died. After the funeral, my father remarked that he'd learned more about his wife in the previous three days of mourning celebrations than he had in the entire time they were married. He would always say she was smarter than he was and I would think, "You're just as smart as mom. You have musical talent. You are an artist and can draw and paint extremely well. You can fix cars and anything else. You invent things." So, I don't know why he thought she was smarter.

In high school, the family moved and I became, of all things, the class clown as a bridge to the strangers with whom I now attended school. Along the way, I earned my God and Country award and made Eagle Scout. That's about all I remember of high school.

Once, when I was an adult, I returned to my childhood home. Out bounded a neighbor eager to reconnect. He launched into the retelling of how he had stopped my father from hitting me with a two by four. Animated and still clearly pleased with his own heroics, he told a story of saving me. Shockingly, I had absolutely no recollection of that story. I cannot recall my father trying to hit me.

For years, religious scientists have tied the emotions to religious awakening. In my life, God defies those studies. God came to me through other means. As shut down as I was, my spirit was apparently alive and well and soaking in God's presence in a way that my emotions could not register. God came to me through the liturgy.

The Episcopal Church was the first spiritual home for me. My family had in fact helped to build it. It was started as an outreach to the college women in town. The group first met in one of the campus buildings. Having outgrown that, everyone pitched in to purchase a pre-fabricated church. The first families were close because everyone had worked together to build the church building. The choir also felt like a family. Since my father participated in the choir, every summer all the choir families took a trip to the conductor's second home in upstate Massachusetts.

As part of my participation in church, I became an acolyte. I took my responsibilities very seriously and I enjoyed them all. I was in my own little world serving the Lord. I don't remember being friends with any of the other boys or expecting the vicar or the acolyte leader to acknowledge me. Of course, with my emotional closure and isolation, it's quite possible they were and did!

Mostly, my memories of church are different than the household family memories. The remembrances have depth and passion to them and I can recall the weekly worship experiences. When I think of those times, I feel a sense of peace.

I remember the choir following me carrying the cross because they had to wait until I was in place. I felt the importance of people relying on me to keep the service going in order. I don't remember feeling scared or the center of the focus. It seemed like the focus was on God so I just melted into the framework. Sometimes it got hard on the knees since there was no cushion for kneeling at the altar.

What I remember best was being close to the elements. They had real wine and the wafers that melted in your mouth. I would carefully retrieve each silver box of wafers from its holding place, then the big silver wine goblet. Next, I would help the vicar wash his hands and hand him the towel to dry them. It was a very intimate ritual. It was like I was the priest too, only I didn't have to speak. I thought, "Isn't God amazing using a useless little kid like me? Wow!"

I loved my prayer book. The inscription says I received the book when I was confirmed, on April 13, 1962. I cannot remember being confirmed. Written on the front cover is the word "Prayer". I had no idea how powerful that one word would become in my life.

The other two objects that meant something to me were pictures of Jesus. One was on a key chain; a beautiful sterling silver picture of the head of Jesus. It was somewhat sculpted, not flat.

I don't know who gave it to me. The other object was even more special to me; a picture of Jesus the shepherd with a lamb atop his shoulders. Again, I don't know where I got it, but I remember deciding to hang it on the headboard of my bed. Fastening a string to it, I tied it to the headboard where it would move as I did.

Staring at it, I recall how I folded my hands to pray. I think the fact I remember praying is significant.

Tom's High-School picture

Completing my degree in college, I headed for the Northwest; six uneventful days across Canada by rail save for one moment in Jasper, when I argued with a train conductor to not remove my cat with the same name. Six days of eating just Cheez Whiz; no crackers, just cheese whiz, and on the seventh day, I celebrated and ate a hot dog. It is an austerity few would voluntarily yield to, let alone design for a lifestyle. Out of the roots of my childhood, such deprivation was a natural. The scar of that trip remains and to this day, I still cannot eat Cheez Whiz!

Soon after arriving in the Northwest, I found myself at a singles group. Lured by the opportunity to play volleyball, and the Lord giving me the ability to play tennis, when I walked in the room with the singles group, I remarked to myself, "They are really glad I'm here." It was a very loving group and I wanted what they had.

I did not know they were praying for me to accept the Lord. I only knew that after some time, I wanted to give my life to Jesus. However closed I was emotionally; I knew Him and His love were real. At a full Gospel breakfast, the question was asked, "Do you want to receive Jesus as your Lord and Savior?" I stood and gave my life to him. The group was overjoyed and my life changed forever. One of the women there was Ruth.

Beyond the basic tools of the books is spiritual agreement. Scripture has promised that where two or three are gathered, there is the presence of the living Christ. For us to be called to a ministry of intercessory prayer, the seeds of that agreement had to be revealed and watered. To intercede for others is to join in agreement with God's purposes for those people.

The holy pact, the covenanted relationship God designs for such ministry begins with a commitment to it. Speaking to our hearts, God drew us to a conference lead by Derek Prince, an advocate of world change through intercession.

The conference was held in one of those cavernous multi purpose rooms so popular in churches in the seventies; rooms that alternately served several hundred for dinner or, if the carefully tucked away basketball hoops descended, could host a church sports league.

Although Ruth and I were participating in the same singles group, we had not really gotten to know each other. We attended separately, seated in two different sides of the room. The speaker's crisp, articulate British speech implored the audience at the end of the evening to consider a commitment to intercessory prayer. If anyone there felt they could commit their hearts to that ministry, they were to stand.

We were there for different reasons. Ruth was there because of years of commitment to exposing herself to those experiences that would generate spiritual growth and maturity. I was there because, out of my new relationship with Jesus Christ, I was hungry for the deep things of God.

We both stood.

Spurred by the new commitment, at Bible Study the next week, Ruth suggested to the group something that had been on her heart for a long time; prayer partners. Since she was a child gathering the neighborhood children around her at the mission dormitory, her deepest desire had been for a prayer partner.

Everyone agreed it was a good idea. We all wrote our names on slips of paper and deposited them in a bowl. As we pulled names out, God's plan began to unravel. Disappointingly, one person chose another's name but a third person chose that person's name. It wasn't going to work. Then the two of us reached in and pulled out... each other's names. Of all the names selected that night, we were the only two who drew each other's names. It was startling.

Now it's possible to look back and see how God had drawn us together since our childhood. Then, we were walking by faith.

Such an astonishing development as the perfectly paired names needed to be honored with obedience. It was not our righteousness or good works, or Biblical knowledge or sound doctrinal thinking that compelled us to the path of being prayer partners, it was our faithfulness. Each of us had, in our own way, responded over and over again to the call of God. Incrementally we had arrived in that living room. Just as we had followed God step by step from the Philippines and New England to the Northwest, we were now joined together to follow God step by step into the lives of others; into the heart and purpose of intercessory prayer.

Though unevenly matched in the number of years we had each known the Lord, we were perfectly matched in our desire to know more of God. We were both willing to open ourselves up to however much God wanted to reveal to us.

We belong to a God who calls us. We are marked from childhood. God marks all of us. The less we struggle and the more we free Him to do his work through us, the better. God has prepared us for the things He will ask us to do. God is always there and it is always by his Grace. God is full of surprises that go against convention. He wants our full-undivided attention and his fingerprints are all over our lives.

We knew the Lord, we acknowledged the sovereignty of God in our history, and we embraced the chance to go deeper.

Ruth had lead enough Bible Studies to know that we needed to begin our times of prayer with a scripture on which to meditate and I trusted her wisdom. This was how we came to start with the devotions.

We fell into a rhythm. Both of us had jobs that began early in the morning. By the time we left for work, we had completed our daily ritual of bringing our prayers to the Lord. From the very beginning we knew we had been called to something special.

Prayer is the most unbelievable gift; it's a set of contradictions. It's the most intimate and also the most far-reaching act. It is the closest thing in your heart and it is touching the thing that is farthest away. It is ultimate joy and profound moments of doubt. It pierces through the veil and it's the closed door of denial. It is the excitement of finding out something new about yourself. It is watching a person transform before your eyes. By the grace of God they are changing. It is touching God. It is sensing his presence and hearing him call your name.

The Ballad of My Animated Tree
By Ruth Vega (Christmas 2001)

There once was an aspiring Christmas tree who was thrown
In a heap, separated from her peers who had the perfect form.
Discarded and lonely, she was dumped among piles of cut up branches,
Who from a family named "Noble Fir" with lovely and thick eye lashes.

Not understanding this treatment, her heart was broken and bent,
She was ready to do away with herself lest, she to the fireplace be sent.
When along came Tootie* with excitement in her voice.
"Lani, over there, that odd-looking tree, that's my choice!"

The tree jumped, unbelievingly, and awoke from despair,
Stirred to hoping, to be chosen and taken…should she dare?
To be decorated, lighted and admired by all!
To stand tall in a living room, den, or even a hall!

The night was dark and dank, no stars in the sky,
Tree could not see for her eyes were no longer dry.
Tears came flowing with anticipation and longing
For this "voice" to follow through what it was actually saying.

Discussion ensued, whether there was room
To salvage this tree from a life of doom.
But Tootie, not bearing to hear its mournful cry
Decided this tree was not meant to die.

She saw the symbols the tree regally bore;
Instead of one pointed branch at the top, there were more!
There sprouted three straight ones looking up!
With arms flailing here and there! Her messages wouldn't stop!

*Pet name for Ruth from her grand children

I'll leave it up to your sensitivity, my friends,
To reveal to you the message my little tree sends.
With paradigm shed, and laughter be had,
Would that if you could, _____ with me, this unique tree.

Animated Tree. Tom said, "It reminds me of who I was before I met Ruth."

FOUR

Ruth and Tom's Life of Prayer

> "How awesome you are dear Father to allow
> us to feel your presence when
> two or three are gathered together in
> your name." Amen
> Matthew 18:20

Ruth:

Because of the two verses- Ephesians 1:3 and 2 Peter 1:4 that were definitely given to both Tom and I, our ministry was **FIRST AND FOREMOST** from the Lord. We had to be grounded and rooted in what those two Scriptures are all about. If we do not have that strong belief, our ministry is not what will give God the glory.

Before we knew it, people were sharing what was happening in their lives after we had prayed for them. Filled with excitement, we decided to start writing the answers down. Thus began the notations in our Bibles and devotional books.

Taking it day by day, our prayer partnership grew. Nine months after we had begun, another confirmation of God's anointing on our ministry was revealed. I told Tom on October 7, 1976 that my morning verse was Ephesians 1:3

"Blessed be the God and Father of our Lord Jesus Christ, who has blessed us in Christ with every spiritual blessing in the heavenly places in Christ…"

To the astonishment of both of us, Tom told me, "That's the verse I chose too!"

The truth and meaning of those words were like a banner carried in front of our ministry. God was indeed blessing us and leading us into heavenly places. The burgeoning record of answered prayer was evidence of God's divine call on our ministry.

The NIV Study Bible has a footnote that says of this verse, "…through their union with the exalted Christ, Christians have already been made beneficiaries of every spiritual blessing that belongs to and comes from the heavenly realm."

To us, the verse, and the mutual choice of it was a mandate for continuing our prayer ministry. It was the unmistakable, clear, no questions asked, intervention of God. It was like God speaking out of the clouds. It doesn't get any better than that. We were committed to moving forward into the heavenly places the Lord was preparing for us: places where people knew we would take their concerns to the throne of God on their behalf.

My years of experience lead me to teach Tom that it was necessary to empty ourselves before we began to pray. We don't start with praying, we start by emptying ourselves. We are not thinking of what to pray ourselves. We don't know what to pray. We say to God, "I only see bits and pieces. You see the bigger picture." It's not my job, when I pray, to tell God what to do. I don't know what God's plans are for the people we're praying for. We ask the Lord for the prayers and who to pray for. This is a process we don't have any control over. We're just trying to tune into God's frequency. God wants us to have a contrite heart to do this work. We are constantly dying seeds being put in the soil, dying to our old ways, so we can grow in the Lord.

Things that are delinquent, in yourself, God will use in the praying and in the lives of other people He brings before you. God gives you guidance on what should be your attitude. The Holy Spirit guides and directs us and connects us with the people we are to pray for. If we are praying after emptying our hearts, ourselves, then we can pray without an agenda. Divine insight will just come to us.

The emptying process always involves the deepest sharing of our hearts, issues from our days at work, offenses taken and given, concerns, worries, or irritations. All of it must be purged. We call it, 'clearing the decks'.

Tom:

At the time we began praying together, I was working in a place I detested. I was employed as a draftsman, and my desk was isolated in the back of a big warehouse. A co-worker insisted on routinely calling me derogatory names. The business practices of the company were marginally ethical. Only complaining seemed to be a way to handle the stress of it.

One day as I was protesting about God's choice of employment for me, Ruth countered me with a new spin on our newly discovered scripture. She pointed out to me that my job was perfect for me at that stage of my faith. It was a *heavenly place.*

As a draftsman, my job was somewhat routine. It did not require all of my thought process to be fully engaged. My desk was in a place where ambient noise would not disturb others. She encouraged me to turn on the radio and find Christian programs that would be edifying to my faith. I could do the work my boss wanted and needed me to do and, at the same time, learn the things of the Lord. Ruth was right. I could catch up on all that I had missed. It *was* a heavenly place.

Soon, I had a schedule of Christian programs I listened to throughout the day. Then I began bringing in tapes as well. My work became not only God's provision to meet my physical needs, but my spiritual needs as well. My attitude changed from resentment and bitterness to gratitude and enthusiasm for the opportunity God had provided.

Throughout the years we discovered the Lord leading us to a variety of heavenly places. There were those places, like my work situation, where we were in a location where the Lord was teaching us through our service or work; a tight spot where dependency on the Lord was the only light on the path. Or we were reaching down and lifting up others who were not so far along the path in their knowledge of God, or faith walk or awareness of God's presence in their life. More often than not, the heavenly places were fresh opportunities to grow in faith as we followed the Holy Spirit in service.

Our ministry quickly became about living in heavenly places; blessed spiritually because of our relationship with God through Jesus Christ. We also met those we served in *their* heavenly places and called them to higher ground or kept them company and offered encouragement along the way as they too grew in their relationships.

Two months later, on December 26, 1976, we picked the same verse again. This time it was II Peter 1:4

"Whereby are given unto us exceeding great and precious promises: that by these ye might be partakers of the divine nature, having escaped the corruption that is in the world thru lust."

Not only was it akin to receiving a mission statement from God for us and our ministry, it was also a reminder, an indication; of the different path our lives would have taken without the gift of our prayer partnership.

Both of us acknowledged that had we not been obedient to the call of God to pray and serve together, we would have ended up in a series of disastrous marriages. By calling us to pray God had lead us away from the weaknesses in our relationship skills at that time. He had led us away from the opportunity to work out our deficiencies by choosing wrong partnerships. Instead, in the process of prayer, He provided us the chance to bring ourselves before Him. He allowed us to empty ourselves and permit Him to present service to God as the arena for maturing neediness into the wealth of His glorious spiritual riches.

The first part of the scripture pointed to the confirmation that we had not chosen this path but rather were called. The second was a roadmap for spiritual maturity. We had our marching orders.

Ruth:
Our routine was beginning to grow and develop. The step we called "clearing the decks" moved to new, deeper levels. I needed to share things with Tom that was bothering me about our personal friendship. Tom also began to need to ask me about what I meant by certain things I had said or done. We began to frequently off load such issues in an effort to get ready to pray in the morning. We would share anything that might be happening to us, or what might get in the way of receiving what God had for us during prayer. Whether it was something between the two of us, or in our work, family or social lives, we talked until we had reached a resolution and that cleared it away. The deepening of emptying ourselves deepened the opportunities for resting in the presence of the Lord.

Today the process remains the same. Once free of, as Tom puts it, the undergrowth, and our interval of prayer begins with silence. The emptying gives way to that Holy tranquility that gently yields to the reverie born when the human spirit opens to God. Praise follows. We always break the silence with praise. We praise who God is and what He does. Giving all glory to God, we acknowledge His sovereignty and mercy. We pray His presence will be supreme in all we do and say. We pray even our mistakes would glorify God as people see them righted. We pray we would see the good in whatever dire situation into which we are called. We pray for Grace.

We sit again in silence and listen. And then the prayers of intercession come, from the heart of God. If you are looking for a formula, there is none. Our time of prayer is a by-product of living with God at the center of our world. We are looking up to Him, knowing we are the spokes on the wheel and He is the center.

We are passionate about our faith and the people for whom we pray. The Spirit quickens us. We have seen the things God does in the lives of the people for whom we intercede and we are excited about it for them. Instead of the burden one might suspect would accompany such intensity, it is a feeling of lightness. We share in the freedom and victory of those for whom we pray.

Sometimes when we pray, we discern the prayer has already been answered. Other times when we pray, we discern the wheels or resolutions are in motion but God would like us to pray anyway. There are also times we are praying for people we do not know and never hear what happened, simply relying on the trust God places in us because someone has brought this person to our attention and requested supplication.

For us, the litmus test of the presence of the Holy Spirit in our intercessions is simple. If what we are praying about comes to fruition, the Spirit is in it. When it's supposed to happen, it's going to. If it's just from us, it won't happen. In so saying, one must not have the impression we pray only for tangible events. The content of our invocations ranges from specific requests, a change of heart, and to only that God's will be done.

Sometimes our way of prayer is not understood. There was, in fact, a time that caused great consternation with a friend because we were not specific in our prayers as she wished. She was hungry to become pregnant and asked us to pray for her conception. We did not feel so led and instead prayed for God's will. When no pregnancy occurred there was a hard place between us. Steadfastness to that which we felt led to pray remained. We prayed the friendship would heal. Slowly, the rift was closed.

Another time, a friend called for a request for her father to pass quickly after a traumatic illness. Again, we felt lead to pray only for God's will. The father rallied and had several days of meaningful kinship before again succumbing to the illness and passing on. They were precious, peaceful days of sharing.

As the word of the nature and purpose of our prayer partnership spread, we began to allow ourselves to be drawn deeply into the lives of the people for whom we were praying. Little things like my love of growing roses gave way to big things like hospital visits and offering our homes to people who needed a place to stay. Hosting Bible Studies gave way to cooking for unexpected visitors. We call it, 'putting legs to our prayers.'

Prayer gives you the confidence to serve others. It is a springboard. When you open up your heart to God, people sense the sincerity when you serve them. It's not the way you talk or what you do, it's who you are. You reveal yourself and the God that has changed your heart. One of the fruits of prayer is a sense of being bonded with the people you pray for.

Being God's people in God's place at God's time has been a hallmark of the 'prayers with legs'. Setting aside our own agenda and claiming our ministry for the Glory of God, became paramount.

Central to this understanding is our belief that all circumstances come from God. While listening to the still small voice as an impetus to service is important, equally important is the observation of circumstances. The internal nudge of the Spirit and the audible voice of God in one's heart coupled with good solid Bible Study offer central direction.

The people who cross our path have been put there by God. The intersection of our lives with the lives of others is, we believe, a heavenly place orchestrated by God. In every circumstance we look to see in what way God is revealed, as well as, the revelation of God's ultimate purpose. We listen not only with our ears but also more with our hearts. God's gift is what we would like to think, or call discernment. To us, circumstances are the visible presence of God. They are an invitation from God to bring His love and mercy to people's lives.

We have never imposed our own assessment of someone's place along the path of spiritual growth over the desire to be God's servants. Our stead is to be obedient to the Holy Spirit through prayer. The rest is God's concern. The verse that spurs us on is found in Ephesians 2:10 "For we are His workmanship, created in Christ Jesus for good works, which God prepared beforehand, that we should walk in them."

The heavenly places and heavenly calling we have experienced and worked to establish in our own daily lives at the beginning has become the foundation for host of other opportunities. Early on in our ministry we had no idea, the adventure had only just begun.

The Lord has such a big kingdom of people with so many different attitudes and different backgrounds. When we pray, we're united in the Spirit. The people God put in our lives have been gifts to us. Praying *for* people is a wonderful privilege. Praying *with* people is a joy. You can keep your life situations, your problems and challenges to yourself, but you miss the blessing of sharing it with someone. To share our burdens and then share the answers to our prayers adds to our understanding of God's love and mercy for us. Galatians 6:2 says: "Bear one another's burdens, and so fulfill the law of Christ."

> *"We're together again, just praising the Lord.*
> *We're together again, in one accord.*
> *Something good is going to happen,*
> *Something good is in store.*
> *We're together again, just praising the Lord."*

Singing this song together with our friends before Bible Studies and prayer meetings and times of fellowship, the words describe the common feature of each group; the togetherness, unity, expectation and praise. During the early years of our prayer partnership, when polyester, plaid bell-bottoms and big hair followed protests and flower power, our home base was a group called "Single Christians Interdenominational Fellowship"(SCIF). A woman recently widowed founded the group. The participants were like her, widowed, or divorced, or had never been married. She felt the institutional church had not provided a place for singles. It was her vision to do so. On Sunday mornings, before we worshipped at our respective churches, the group met for study and prayer at various restaurants; first one and then, when we outgrew that one, another. As a group, we consciously decided to focus on the spiritual and not the dating aspect of fellowship. We were going to be family; brothers and sisters in Christ.

If you decided to bring a date, it had to be a 'package deal'. There were no pairs. You shared your date with others. No one was to show their affections in the group. I really fought for that. Because we were all different ages, it was important. The Lord gave us a verse for the group.

"God gives the desolate a home to dwell in; he leads out the prisoners to prosperity; but the rebellious dwell in a parched land." (Psalm 68:6)
Another translation says, " *God sets the solitary in families*"

The study soon grew into fellowship activities. We would get together on Friday night for volleyball and then go out to eat afterwards. Again, even in aspects such as our rules for volleyball was found the inclusiveness, which was so important to us. The ball must be hit three times before it went over the net. One of those hits had to be a woman.

By Saturday we couldn't wait to see each other again. After breakfast together, we would go on hikes or to the movies. Any excuse we could find to get together would be carried out. We even took vacations together. One member moved to the Bahamas for a while and, of course, we *had* to visit. The pictures recording the trip show a beaming group, on the beach, clearly devoted to each other.

The group became more intimately constructed. A telephone number was available so people could call if they needed help, were lonely, afraid, or wanted to get people together for an activity. The group grew in mutual affection for the Lord and each other.

The activities fell together naturally. There were "Do It Yourself Classes" in which a person could learn a new skill. "Rhythm Nights" were musical extravaganzas when whole families, thereby including the singles with children, would come together to teach each other dances, sing songs, or play instruments.

Work parties were a fun way to get moving since it brought us alongside one another to lift and load. Gardening, housework, anything heavier than one person could do alone was welcomed as a chance to support each other and love each other in the Lord.

After we completed the work, we'd all go out and celebrate with ice cream.

Often during the work parties, Tom and I were the only ones that would show up consistently. For us, it was another confirmation of our partnership. As we worked alongside each other, we got to know each other better. It was God's unique training program for what lay ahead.

Soon enough, that season of training was over. Others began to join us again. During one particular work party, a woman named Marilyn was there. She and I began to work on washing windows at a housecleaning party. With Marilyn on one side of the window and I on the other, we joked and laughed our way through the chore. It was the beginning of a great and abiding friendship. Tom and I were prayer partners, but Marilyn, Tom, and I were the Three Musketeers of Christian Fellowship. With three strikingly different personalities, we each brought remarkably different perspectives to each activity and study. Together we lead each other to a deep relationship with the Lord. Since, as Marilyn says, "Faithfulness breeds faithfulness", the strength of the friendship brought us all into more heavenly places.

Eventually, Tom realized he was in love with Marilyn. If every pot has a top, she was it for him. It seemed the perfect situation. We could continue to be prayer partners, and Tom would know the deepest richest relationship with Marilyn. He gathered his courage and asked her to marry him. To his shock, Marilyn said no. The next two years consisted of Tom not talking to her, or wanting to be around her, throwing a divisive pitch into our three-way friendship. Although he never stopped being in love with her, he was able to eventually accept her rejection. Today the friendship has returned and our triune prayers remain strong as ever despite the fact that Marilyn has moved from the area. Returning for occasional visits, we pick up where we left off every time we all three see each other. Such is the proof, once more, of God's sovereignty in all relationships where Jesus is Lord.

The singles group in due time lapsed into inactivity. Its moment in the seasons of God's nurture had ceased. The anointing was gone and the group disbanded. Today members live across the nation, but we stay in touch through e-mails and phone calls. God's touch through the experiences remains a living presence.

As a minority, I had been refused the teaching positions in nicer schools with middle class children. God has given me the will to take adversity and surrender it to His glory. I took the challenge and ran with it. I began as a teacher by taking on the tough classes no one could deal with. Again and again, I worked to show the officials and the children themselves, they could achieve a new level of success.

Years of that history led to earning a spot at a suburban elementary school. There I found, among others, two new strong Christian friends; the school secretary, and the office assistant. We were all believers in the power of prayer. For more than a decade, we walked together and prayed together. Once again, the communal power of prayer powered the removal of mountains and blessed our lives.

The school secretary's husband had MS. It was a heavy burden and, much to my amazement, time and again unbeknownst to me, I was led by the Holy Spirit to find just the right word of encouragement to come out of my mouth, or I would drop by for a visit. One time, I even showed up in full clown regalia complete with make up to cheer him up. It is fun following the Spirit.

The three of us prayed as the diagnosis was first being determined. Doctors were unable to determine what disease he suffered and we continued to pray for a diagnosis.

In God's own way, my secretary friend was sitting in a doctor's waiting office reading a magazine that happened to list the symptoms of MS. Until that point, the doctors were wavering and cogitating with various options, not sure of her husband's symptoms. She recognized her husband's symptoms were identical to the list in the magazine. When their turn came, they entered the doctor's office to talk to him. The doctor expounded the mystery of determining the illness. Suddenly, her husband spoke up. "She knows what I have. I have MS." She showed the doctor the article that quickly set up the next round of tests. My friend knew it was the power of prayer that had led her to the article when the doctors were stymied.

Prayer continued to be the source of strength and encouragement during the duration of the disease. At one point, her husband wanted to go to the Philippines because there were reports of a miracle healing. Desperate to get well, he was ready to put his family in financial jeopardy to do so. She brought the prayer concern to us. Earnestly we prayed and it was revealed the healing was a hoax and her husband, although disappointed, changed his plans. Once again, prayer had changed life's direction for the good of all involved.

My friend, the office assistant also found strength in the prayer partnership. The encouragement the group gave to her as they prayed for her made an enormous difference in her life.

Her brother always seemed to make the wrong choices. He had three unsuccessful marriages, was drinking, and his kids were a constant source of heartache. The little group started praying for him and things started turning around. Today he is sober, has a good job and is partnered with a wonderful woman in a committed relationship.

Over and over we found our prayers answered and God listening to and being active in our lives. Together we bore the burdens of our lives, sharing the journey and enjoying the God given community that happens when people pray in agreement. Beyond ourselves, we prayed for the students, parents, and staff of the school. Prayer was the constant source of strength, encouragement and surrender.

I worked under several principals. One in particular was very hard on me and the situation was a real trial. On one of our regular walks around Greenlake, Tom and I prayed I would just release the situation to God and stop worrying about it. The next morning, the principal told us before school started that she had decided to retire. Ah! The mystery of God's timing as we surrender our hearts to him and his sovereignty.

Another part of my prayer life during that time was for my curriculum ideas. God had given me the idea to forge some friendships with older people at my mother's retirement home. I paired each of my students with a senior. All year long they would write to each other. At the end of the year, we would visit. Everyone met their pen pal and the students would perform some musical numbers. It was wonderful experience.

Out of that adventure, I discovered the nursing home, nearby, was looking for someone to do music with the residents. I started a sing-a-long group centered around the good old hymns and some scripture. When it became necessary for me to pass that ministry on, God provided the perfect couple to take over the leadership. One of them, Jeanette, is a proficient accordion player. We still stay in contact with each other and continue to pray for the residents.

Beyond my prayers with my good friends in the office, I found others with whom Tom and I could pray. The calling of being a teacher was a common bond that drew people past building boundaries. Having made friends with one colleague, Mame, early on, she continued to call me with prayer requests for her students even when our careers separated us. Theologically, Mame had come from a tradition more about pleasing some objective God, almost as an idol, than pleasing the Lord in a relationship. The act of teaming up with Tom and I to pray afforded her the opportunity to experience our relationship with the Lord and deepen hers. A tremendously gifted teacher, we consider it, still, a gift to have prayed with her.

Now that I've retired from teaching, I look back on those years as times of rich fellowship and the visible movement of the Lord in response to prayer. All praise to our living God!

Tom:

For me as well, work was a source of opportunities to live out and witness to my faith through prayer and study. God had moved me from my 'heavenly place' and landed me a job with a major aerospace company in the area. The move had come, of course, from prayer.

One night at our Christian bible study, the Lord spoke to my heart, saying, "Ask the group to pray for you to get a new job and I will give it to you." Fortunately, at the end of the study, we had prayer and Royal, a member of the group, remembered to pray for me to land a new job. A very short time afterwards, my landlord came over to my apartment.

I mentioned in passing I was looking for a new job. The landlord knew of an opening in his own group at this aerospace company. The job was for a mechanical draftsman, something for which I had both training and experience. Within days, I had been interviewed and hired from the inside track. What I didn't know was that God was giving me an assignment as well as a job.

The aerospace industry is, by the nature of all businesses, interested in what people can do for their profit margin. It is not a place that is given to relationships or personal concerns. Thus it was that God brought six of us men together for lunchtime Bible Study. We needed to get together, sit down and encourage each other. We would read verses and talk to each other about personal and family agendas. Each lunch was closed in prayer for each other.

Tom and his lunch-time Bible study group.

The experience of the men in the Christian faith was broadly defined. From one of the guys, Thomas, who had gone to seminary, to a young man, Preston who was not yet a Christian, they represented the complete spectrum of the Christian experience.

Preston had come to the Bible Study to ask lots of questions. Soon he accepted the Lord and was very enthusiastic about his faith. Thomas was very conservative theologically. Nonetheless, on the heels of the new convert's ebullience about the things of the Lord, Thomas and another gentlemen went with Preston to a charismatic Episcopalian church. All three of them experienced the baptism of the Holy Spirit.

Preston then began to evangelize to a friend, Wayne, who accepted the Lord. The group began to pray for the conversion of his mother. She accepted the Lord. His sister was next on the list! I'm still waiting to hear the end of the story.

While the corporate concerns were putting planes in the air, God's business was to put wings on prayers. God granted great favor to the movement of Christians in the company during that time. A newsletter was developed and circulated to several hundred people. One of the believers was a projectionist for the company. The Christian fellowship began to show Christian films such as "How Should We Then Live?" by Francis Schaeffer. In the company's theater, forty five minutes at a time, at the heart of the day, Christians were meeting to be taught, and encourage each other, then returning to our cubicles and places on the line refreshed with the knowledge of who we were and to whom we belonged. If someone complained to the management, we decided we would just stop showing the films. We prayed we wouldn't be interrupted or shut down. The films continued.

Our small group prayed for the company as well. When, the corporation was really struggling, the Bible Study prayed earnestly for an increase in work. Within a short time, a large unexpected contract came in. Everyone was very surprised and filled with joy. The Lord was using a small group of ordinary men to bring His presence into a giant corporation that was least of all concerned with having a soul let alone the Spirit. And we were courageous enough, out of our love for the Lord and desire to serve, to be obedient to the impulse of the Holy Spirit.

For three years, the Lord's community was present and praying at that company. Eventually, transfers began to break up the group.

Ruth:
At the close of the Vietnam War, I had the opportunity to give my testimony about being a refugee from the Philippines during

World War II. I shared how difficult it had been for me coming to this country alone during such a time of crisis. Agencies such as the Red Cross could be helpful, I told them, but relationships with people who are helping without getting paid to do so are the life changing experiences. Refugees need to feel the love of Christian people.

I explained to the audience my prayer was for something we could do beyond prayer. I was looking for legs for those prayers.

After my talk, a woman came up to me to tell me her husband was a senator. God's answer to my prayer was set in motion.

Soon there was a budget to devise a summer program. With my training as an ESL teacher, I was able to devise a program assisting refugees in their independence from public services. I found a local Catholic Church willing to host us. One of the other churches in the area agreed to let us use their gym for sports activities. I recruited Marilyn and Tom and others for volunteer tutors. Dividing the group by ages, we were on the way.

In addition to our studies, I would give the group pep talks explaining to them that they were not entirely helpless. "Look at me," I would say. "I did it and you can too. It took me years, but it is possible to adjust." I passed on helpful hints. "Listen to the radio and imitate the speech to practice your pronunciation," I told them. I encouraged them to watch body language to assist them in knowing what people were saying. Always I reminded them there were people out there who loved them.

Field trips were added to the basic program. We would take several cars and go look for important signs. We would visit the refugees' homes. We offered help with domestic situations. If there were youth in the country alone with family back in Vietnam, we would bring them particularly close, helping them stay in school and supporting them so they were not lonely. Preoccupied with the safety and care of their family far, far away, the support helped the youth stay focused and accomplishing their goals. The program ran a full summer. Everyone had a wonderful time and learned a lot.

The program was renewed for a second year. More refugees from all over the world enrolled; Laotian, Japanese, Hispanic, and Eastern European.

Years later, I discovered how strong the cords of God's love were in that group. The secretary from the elementary school where I worked had a son who married one of the ESL students. The young girl still referred to me as "her teacher." God is always drawing people together.

There were times when we were part of groups we were not leading. One such group was a Bible Study and Choir that came out of members of a local Roman Catholic Church. The founder, Julie, was a 'cradle Catholic' that had, by her own report, never read a Bible.

In 1986, a secular class she was supposed to attend had been canceled. Riding in the car with a friend, they were deciding where they should go and how they should spend the time now that they had free time. Remembering the announcement of a prayer class being held that day at a local seminary, she and her friend decided that would be their destination for the day.

Walking into the room seeing people lifting their hands and singing praises, Julie thought to herself 'These people are nuts'. But the day left an impression on her. Spiritual hunger continued and grew. One day, someone riding the bus with her commented to her, "You have time for everything. There is time for prayer and study." That comment planted a deep seed.

My life had begun to cross paths with Julie's and in that crossing I invited her to attend a Tuesday night Bible Study. Out of that, Julie decided to start a Friday night prayer meeting that I began to attend. The fellowship in that group transcended denominational boundaries. The experiences in the evening group grew as people frequented classes offered at the church, which was the social hub of the community. The blessing of spiritual maturity continued as we prayed for young and old, single and married.

One woman's daughter suffered from a terrible extended fever that would not be reduced until the group started praying. The fever broke and the daughter was restored to full health with no ill after effects.

We prayed for inner healing and in those prayers, Tom was ministered to in a great and mighty way, by being delivered of much of his 'baggage'.

There were adventures with that group as well, putting legs to our prayers. One of the members had a relative who was serving on a ship that had come to port. Knowing these young men had been at sea without Filipino food for some months, I invited the gang of them for a feast to be shared and hosted by the prayer group. All had a grand time. The boys went back to ship and set to sea not only with stomachs filled with their native food but new clothes on their backs some members had donated.

Unexpectedly, someone on board had a medical emergency. Back came the ship to port. This time, the young male relative decided he wanted to jump ship and stay in our city. I laughed and told him I did not think God was calling me to harbor a fugitive. Reluctantly he returned to the ship. Wisdom is part of His service!

My experience with the prayer group led me to sing with the Filipino choir. Several in the group were members. The opportunities to bring God's influence continued, as I became their prayer leader. Remember the red dress on my Catholic confirmation day? The Lord will make a way where there is no way that we might serve where and when he wants.

Tom, too, grew through the strong association with the Filipino community. Somewhat of an 'orphan' because of his faith walk and the ways it separated him from his family, he was adopted into a new culture and gained new 'family' that added richly in his life as he participated in weddings, and funerals and feasts celebrations.

As with Tom's deliverance from some childhood issues, with the Friday night prayer group, I too was to discover a layer of deep healing I needed. The comfort I felt in the common ground of being with people from my culture was a stark contrast to another group with which I was associated.

In the beginning of the nineteen eighties, I became involved in a Christian Women's political caucus. The conferences held by the organization were particularly difficult for minority women because our needs were not being addressed. Others did not seem to understand that life was much more difficult for women of color. The Caucasian women did not, and apparently could not, grasp what life was like for us. Plagued with a high fever and flu like symptoms, there was one conference I forced myself to attend. I felt I *had* to go. The last part of the conference was an altar call. I was called upon to help serve communion. Standing in front, prepared to minister with the elements, suddenly I saw all those white women coming towards me. Memories of what happened in college, the discrimination I suffered with the school district, all the racial hatred and prejudice came flooding forward with the women. Holding those elements, I realized I had to forgive them. Tears began to stream down my face. Drenched in my own spiritual and emotional experience, it was the final healing.

After the service there were solicitations for testimonies. With my heart pounding, I stood and told the group I had found forgiveness. People in the gathering began to cry with me. All the years of war, all the years of prejudice were healed in one moment of service to the community. The God of my life had again gifted me, through the Holy Spirit, with blessing.

When I was little, I was very afraid of the water. In those days in the Philippines, many were taught to swim by being thrown into the ocean. I was one of them. Having been pitched into the waves, I was sick with fear afterwards. My fever would not go down for days. Family members put me in front of a statue of the Virgin Mary — a ritual used only in the direst circumstances — for my well being. In God's time, my health returned. Ironically I was left with a desire to swim.

As an adult, I swam at local pools for my health, but some residual fear persisted. I did not like to swim alone so I attended public sessions. Surrounded by people, it was natural to begin to find people with whom to pray.

At one pool near the school where I was teaching, I began a tradition of Breakfast Potlucks. Everyone would swim early and then all would enjoy the foods each had signed up to bring like muffins, juice, and fruits. Much to my surprise, a columnist for the city newspaper included news when I was retiring from my teaching job, that the 'unofficial social secretary' of the pool was retiring inviting all to a special celebration on my last morning.

Seattle Post-Intelligencer, June 10, 1987 (Jean Godden's column):
Last-minute splash: Ruth Vega overslept and almost missed her own surprise retirement party at the Meadowbrook Pool Friday. Vega, the pool's unofficial social director, is leaving Wedgewood School after teaching 22 years. She's been swimming three mornings a week since November, 1975, when the Meadowbrok morning lap swim began. Noted one of the morning people: "It's hard to recognize everybody with their clothes on.

Moving to another pool closer to home, I, of course, found another group of women with whom to pray. For years, the new group prayed for the one of our member's daughters. She was mentally and emotionally unstable, refusing to stay on her medication. We prayed and prayed with little results. Her mom would bring her food and leave it at her door.

Year's later, when the mother of the daughter died, the Lord's healing was completely visible as the young woman not only attended, but hosted her mother's funeral, stable and alert. Standing at the door after the service, she greeted each person as they left. Our prayers had been answered; a living witness to God's perseverance and timing.

As the Bible studies formed and disbanded over the years, one in particular found not only strength in the fellowship but power in the prayer that brought us all through difficult periods in our lives. A most unusual group put together by God, we were completely diverse. Geographically we had come from all over the world; Hawaii, the mainland, Costa Rica, Philippines, and China. We ranged in age from in our twenties to our fifties. Yet, we had everything in common in the Lord. We shared ourselves and our stories. In that sharing we gained enormous understanding about God. We prayed for extended families and life situations and coworkers and their churches. We learned constantly from each other.

Our name, Meatballs, came from a story akin to the loaves and fishes. One of our members married and at the reception it became apparent that for whatever reason, there were too many meatballs.

We decided we would all take some home. For months, we ate those meatballs. The name stuck. We were henceforth dubbed, "The Meatballs."

The "Meatballs."

It was a logical extension of God's provision. As he was providing edification through his Word and answers through the prayers he put on our hearts, so he had named us...and given us good food!

In that group, I came to know confrontation in a new and exciting way. A forthright group of women, no one was exempt from our observations of behaviors and choices. As the eldest member, seniority gave me no rank. It was the rare experience for me to find those who would not only stand beside me, but also stand up to me. I found it refreshing and challenging.

Like the rest of the groups with whom Tom and I had been intertwined, God's activity was ever present through our prayers. Kathy, a roommate of mine, found solace and peace in nursing her dying mother and, beyond, in her passing. It was a long and difficult time. One night left her bereft of strength. With an urge from the Lord, she called Tom and I and asked us to pray immediately for relief. Peace descended.

Doris made it through a difficult transition. New to the country, she found herself in need of a job shift as at that same time she was facing major health issues. Again, the power of prayer was evidenced in the Grace she felt as she moved through the new doors God was opening.

The same Maria, who refers to our stories as holy, was single and new to Christianity when she started meeting with the group regularly. In the course of time she found herself married with children. By the time the group had begun to meet less regularly the group had prayed her through all the major changes in her life including a time when she and her husband were faced what they believed was a diagnosis of an unborn child with Down's Syndrome. The child was born healthy, but the months until that revelation were long and hard. The prayers of the group sustained her.

Much to Tom's disappointment, since he was the only male, the group decided they preferred he not join our group. We were so lively and faithful it was hard for him to accept. But of course, I brought many of their concerns to our Morning Prayer time, so he was able to have the joy of interceding for them.

Through it all, we Meatballs laughed and cried and shared and encouraged and wept with each other.

I believe that you can keep what is happening in your life a secret and not share it with anyone, but you will miss the opportunity to have a community pray for you, help you, and share in the blessing of answered prayer. That is the gift you will be missing. My prayer for Meatballs recaps exactly what the heart of the Lord intended for our moment in time.

> *"Lord we do have a lot to praise you for. You said to be in Thanksgiving all the time and we are because we have love. We thank you Lord through the years we had together with the Meatballs. We thank you they were not wasted years because they were years spent with you. Years spent in good company and fellowship, community, loving each other celebrating each other's weddings, births and birthdays. We thank you for the opportunity to witness to your bounty and your sovereignty you made all those things happen, you allowed them to happen and you gave us the desire to be together and for the prayers that have gone up to you, that were given by you, that were answered*

by you. We remember how you brought us together and that it was not by chance that this group was formed. The times in which we had confrontation were good for our relationships because they made our relationships stronger. These were our Ebenezers, our mileposts in our spiritual life, which have been made rich because you allowed it to happen. These are memories that will count for eternity because together we walked in our journey, in our search for you. We thank you for them. The glory goes to you; the honor goes to you; not what we have done but the opportunities you gave us and even the desires you gave to us. The prayers, the love, you are the source of all the things we have enjoyed. We know that all these things work together for good because you have taught us to love you and how to love each other. You called us for a purpose. Thank you Lord that your Holy Spirit can guide us."

These prayers are the benediction; not only for the Meatballs, but also for all the groups the Lord led us with which to be involved. They speak to the power of prayer in community as it is lived out in relationships that are a living witness to sustenance and transformation through God's Grace. They speak to the heart of our ministry.

Tom:
As I began to heal, I was able to take on more responsibilities and open myself up to new ministry opportunities. I decided to help out ushering at church. At first I was constantly worried about what might go wrong. The church Ruth and I attend has several thousand members and since being around people made me feel like I was drowning, it was quite a challenge. God showed up as usual. Today I usher with ease. I have developed prayerful friendships with two other ushers. We go out for meals together, pray together and share our lives.

Recently one of us had surgery in another state. I traveled with the other member of the trio to visit for a weekend during the friend's hospital stay. Having extended ourselves well beyond the duties of ushering, we found common ground.

The Lord always uses prayer to draw us into relationship with Him and others. Prayer is about relationships. I grew from a limited ability to relate to initiating and maintaining many relationships through the very act of praying. I was beginning to let the Lord flesh out my own individual life.

Whether big groups or small, long term or short seasons of friendship, Ruth and I have linked hands in prayer with others as they enter God's presence and influence in their lives. Others we pray with throughout our daily walk strengthen the power of our partnership.

The many communities in which we have prayed are the foundation for our intercessions for other people. Gathered with others, we are strengthened to pray for those to whom God has called us to minister.

Ruth:

God has given a wonderful gift to me for people who can't communicate in normal ways. A member of one of the Bible Studies Tom and I attended was afflicted with a burst aneurysm while he and his wife Flo were traveling. Word got back to the Bible study. Praying earnestly, miraculously he was brought back both medically and geographically. Once home, they put him in a good hospital. His recovery was slow at best. He was still having trouble moving his limbs.

Compounding the difficult recovery were other ailments including heart problems. It was a discouraging process. David was a Filipino brother in Christ I had met during college. His situation tugged at my heart in a special way. Regularly, another woman from the Filipino choir and I would visit him and massage his legs.

Meanwhile, David's wife Flo was having difficulty being alone at night. She asked me to stay with her at night. It was not an easy decision for me. Periodically, I cared for my grandchildren and my daughters depended on that care. Concerned with my commitment, I felt the Lord's assurance that if I cared for His spiritual family, He would care for my biological family.

Sure enough, avenues for a flexible care pattern emerged. I was able to stay with her at night and my grandchildren were well cared for. Flo came to the Lord and slipped away many times, but David survived and learned to walk and talk and lived for six more years. The prayers for healing were answered.

The incidence of reaching someone in a semi-conscious state happened again with my godmother. Having had a brain tumor removed, the family was told she was brain dead. Tom and I visited her regularly. Since she was paralyzed, I would massage her legs to repattern the muscles and keep the nerves alive. I told her of the dream I had that she had moved her legs. The dream seemed real.

Sometimes the Filipino choir would sing as well. As the indigenous songs began, much to our amazement, this paralyzed woman would move her big toe to the rhythm! The nurses told us it was just a reflex, but when we stopped singing, the toe stopped moving. There was no doubt about it. She was responding to the music!

In a wonderful way, God led Tom and I to buy condos in the same building, although the purchases were several years apart. I had given my home to my son. A seemingly extravagant gesture, it was necessary for him. It was out of my mother's heart to do so. A friend offered to take me in. Within a short period of time, I had purchased the condo.

Worried constantly about whether I could handle the mortgage payments I vexed myself about the situation until one night I declared to the Lord, "If I have to sleep on a park bench, I will be where you want me to be." Perfect peace descended upon me. Soon after, my son repaid me completely and my worries were a thing of the past.

The purchase of the condo, too, was another of God's interventions. Years earlier, I had come out of the recreation center where I swam frequently. As I gazed casually across the street, I looked at the building and thought to myself, "That would be a good place to live after I retire." Eventually, we were driving by the building. The center includes a huge playground and a large lake with an encircling path. As we pulled up to the stop sign, I noticed a 'for sale by owner' sign. Since it was placed in a third floor window and I was seated on the opposite side of the street, to this day, Tom can't figure out how I saw it.

An attractive relatively low elevation concrete building with lanais dotting the front and a rock garden in the back, we entered the friendly looking little building. To our surprise and delight, the man who owned the condo sold it to me almost on the spot with little legal hassle and no references. Surrender had led to blessing. Several years later, Tom was able to purchase a condo in the same building on a different floor. After renting it out for a few months, he too moved in.

With the new residences, came a whole new group of people for whom to pray. One of them was a lovely woman named Leona.

Leona was always cleaning outside the condo building, or doing something to improve the surrounding area such as planting flowers, weeding, or sweeping. A completely giving woman, she did everything for her husband. I liked her immensely. We shared the chores cheerfully and joyously. I would advocate for her at condo meetings, suggesting she be reimbursed for the purchase of flowers, or I'd commend her for work in some way. She also took me to some mission programs at her church. We were true confidantes.

Leona had successfully fought off cancer once. Now it had come back for a second time. She wasn't doing well. After years of caring for her husband, he was burdened by his own impending loss and not able to care in return. So distraught and in tears, Leona would pretend to sleep when he would come to visit. Sick as she was, she still had to be in the caring role. We visited her regularly. When we called on her, she was lively and interested in all we had to say. I would read the Bible to her and sing her favorite hymn, which was 'Faith of our Fathers.'

As time went by, the cancer began to win. One night, I felt the imperative of the Holy Spirit and called Tom to say we had to go to the hospital right away. Upon arriving, we found her thirsty and dry and close to death. I gave her ice chips as comfort. Soon, the Lord took her home.

At the memorial, I spoke of that great truth that a person always gets more than they give when the Lord asks them to do something. She had such a sweet spirit. She was always teaching me things. She taught me how to die. Even today when I sweep around the condo or work with the flowers, I think to myself, "Leona would be so happy."

I very much enjoyed the special ministry to the dying with which the Lord has blessed me. One such blessing came from a visit to Hawaii.

I had always been curious to go to Hawaii. So it was a gift when a fellow teacher told me she wanted me to fly to Hawaii to meet her family. Before I went, I offered a prayer to the Lord to use me in some way during my visit. I didn't want to just be sightseeing or have a vacation. I offered myself in service.

My first impression on landing was that everybody looked like me. In the States, I was a minority. In Hawaii, I felt like I fit. My friend had nine brothers and sisters.

Bonding with the family was instantaneous and we 'adopted' each other right away. One of the sisters was a Christian and it was arranged that I would stay with her. It was explained that the sister had one son who was a bit peculiar. Grossly overweight, he never came out of his little apartment in the garage and didn't talk to anyone.

I discovered upon my arrival that they had a piano, so I made myself at home and started to play the only piece I knew from memory, "The Scarf Dance" by Chaminade. To everyone's amazement, out of the garage came Walton! Further shocking everyone, he began to tell me that song reminded him of a favorite aunt. There he was, long hair, big tummy, hardly ever attending any family functions, engaging me in conversation. I felt an unusual bond with him.

Throughout the night I kept hearing noises outside on the patio and past the couch where I was sleeping. Later I understood it was Walton and he must have been in pain. I called Tom, even though it was the middle of the night back on the mainland, and asked him to pray for Walton and pray for his mom. It felt like there was something heavy I was supposed to do.

Morning came, and my hostess, Walton's mom, and I went to a prayer breakfast at a local restaurant.

Everyone put his or her prayers in a little container anonymously. Because my paper was slightly open and Walton's mother was collecting them, she saw that I had written 'complete healing, body, mind and soul for Walton.'

Arriving back at home, I went in first. There was Walton lying face down on the floor. His body was still warm. I lifted his hand and prayed, "Into your hands I commend his spirit."

Of course his mother was hysterical when she saw his condition. I called for an ambulance. By the time they came, he had died.

Little did I know, my prayers would be answered in heaven; the most complete healing of body, soul and mind. The night before I had been studying the Bible and found a scripture that said, "I have died to save you and your household." I shared the verse with his distraught mother and it brought her great comfort. Knowing that her faith covered her son brought her the encouragement she needed.

The skirmishes that sometimes erupt around death began. Some people wanted an open casket and some wanted it closed. People began to not speak to each other. Because I was new, I was able to get people to talk to each other and reconcile so they could participate together at the funeral. By the time all was resolved, it was a deeply meaningful ceremony

To this day we are all friends. We visit each other frequently on both sides of the ocean.

My Hawaiian Family (Ruth and Larry) seated

I had been praying for a friend of mine who had just lost her husband to death. At the urge of the Holy Spirit, I called her up and told her I wanted to come over. I told her she didn't have to talk; I just wanted to be there.

When I got to my friend's home, I found her huddled in a corner. I asked her for a fry pan. While the friend sat encased in her grief, I made her egg rolls, which I remembered were her favorite. When I was done cooking I cleaned up and left. For years the friend told everyone how she had been forgetting to eat and I came and cooked her favorite egg rolls. I knew the Lord led me to do exactly that which would show my friend the loving presence of God.

Another friend of mine, also named Ruth, was battling cancer. In the past, she'd taken care of my kids when I really needed help. Hearing she was so sick, I flew to Alaska to help her. I had a plan. My son is a naturopathic Medical Doctor, so I meant to fly her down to my home so she could receive treatments.

It was not what my friend Ruth really wanted. She ended up staying in Alaska where she wanted to be when she passed to be with the Lord.

Tom and I have learned other people's choices are not our responsibility. We are to offer help when we can and bring the Gospel message as an option. That's important to remember in ministering to others. They can choose the path of their desire as God allows.

Sometimes people ask us to pray for material needs. I tell them to get into the Word. When someone is in dire need of something, Tom and I pray, "Lord make them hunger and thirst for the Word. Speak to that person through your Word."

This is what the Lord wants us to do because he wants our attention. It's the trials and tribulations that get our attention. It's those devastating times when he gets our attention. Immersing oneself in the Word is the answer during those times.

Tom:

Ruth excels at trusting the Spirit to lead and work things out. She is perfectly comfortable with the unexpected. So it is not a surprise that one evening, when we stopped for a red light, she followed God's lead to invite a young man named Ernie with his suitcase into her car.

They had established eye contact and he smiled as if he knew her. He reminded Ruth of her oldest son. Though the 'walk' sign had come on for him, he didn't move. Ruth checked with her friend who was riding along to see if she was comfortable with asking him into the car. Agreeing, they rolled the window down and hailed him to the back seat.

Looking in the rearview mirror Ruth noticed his smile had changed to a look of alarm and bewilderment. Ruth told him their names to put him at ease and explained they were on their way to a meeting of their Christian singles group. She asked if he would like to come along. "'Yes," he responded.

After the meeting, Ruth offered to give him a ride to his home. He explained he was visiting from California. Without going into many details, he remarked the place where he had been staying didn't have room for him anymore. She called me to come to her place and take Ernie home to her guest room.

With me, he shared more details. Apparently he hitchhiked aimlessly from California, ending up in Seattle staying with someone whom he only casually knew. For whatever reason, he had been evicted from that place and he never said why. When Ruth showed him where he would be staying he was deeply touched. It had been long time since he had slept in sheets.

The next day, the singles group was holding Bible Study at Ruth's house. Ernie attended and gave testimony that included having once been a Christian but then wandered away from the Lord. In fact, he once sold drugs in the very neighborhood where Ruth now lived. It was quite a change for him. He rededicated his life to the Lord and asked for forgiveness.

All of us in the group prayed for his faith to be strengthened, for his needs to be met, and for guidance about his direction in life. He stayed in touch with Ruth and I as he traveled on. The day came when we received the news that he had entered seminary.

In due time, Ernie became a missionary to Japan. The willingness to invite those outside our sphere of influence, such as Ernie, into God's precious circle of care has translated into transformed lives.

Ruth:

My friend Janet has passed away now. Much to my surprise, while she was alive, she claimed I had led her to the Lord. The truth was, I didn't realize she wasn't a believer. I would just talk to her about my faith and my Bible study as if she already believed.

I assumed we had that in common. Likewise, Janet was a great spiritual and moral support and one of my best friends.

Eventually she did accept the Lord and became one of my prayer partners. Janet had a mother and an aunt who had not talked to each other for thirty years. She went to her pastor and he recommended to not interfere. I had a different perspective. From my knowledge that God is always reconciling, the Bible study prayed for the upcoming Thanksgiving holidays. There always had to be two dinners because the sisters would not be in attendance together. The group told Janet, at the impetus of the Lord, to invite them to the same dinner. She did. To her delight, they started talking to each other and the rift has been healed every since.

Prayer can move that which looks difficult into easy resolution. God's ways are not our ways. If there is no formula to prayer, there is certainly no formula to answered prayer. Tom and I have learned and share with other people that if you are willing to take a risk, the Lord can do mighty things.

Perhaps one of my most difficult situations was with a young Filipino family living here in the States. They had just come to this country. Pregnant with her fifth child, the mother was told by her doctors that the pregnancy would not come to full term and there was a danger of losing her life as well.

Tom and I came to know of the situation through a Bible Study where someone alerted everyone to the need for prayer for this family. I suggested our group go visit them and sing songs.

Already in a coma, the machines registered that she was hearing the praise choruses we were singing and it was having a positive impact. As a charismatic Catholic, she knew all the choruses we were singing.

The older kids were devastated with her condition as she was the head of the household. Her husband was too burdened emotionally to lead them in any way. Our group had gone to their house and done some cooking for them. In the course of those visits, the family decided I was the one to decide for them whether or not to abort the baby and thus save the mother's life. They asked me to step in as translator for them and the doctors as well.

It was not a decision I wanted to make. I talked to everyone I knew about praying for me, for wisdom.

In the end, the baby aborted naturally and I was spared having to make a decision. Unfortunately the mother died as well. Again, I stepped in and helped them with the transition. We still remain in contact to this day. The youngest daughter has just had her first child. It's a blessing to be there for a family in need.

Tom:

At my 'heavenly place' of work, a gentleman named Otto was challenging me. A headstrong German man with a quick temper, he was one of the restaurant salesmen for the restaurant designs I was drafting.

When Otto went into his tirades, the air would be blue with his swearing and it was a shock to my system. As usual, I talked the problem over with Ruth and we prayed about it. Ruth advised me to confront Otto and I couldn't imagine a scarier idea. Ignoring him might be the solution of choice, but never confronting him! Finally I had to do something. To my surprise, out of my mouth came the words, "Otto, Why are you so upset?" Otto stopped dead in his tracks, paused and immediately replied, "It's my wife!"

His anger was the result of being hounded by a problem he couldn't explain or solve. With his frustration out in the open, it lost steam by the minute. He finally calmed down and then came the most miraculous turn of events. I discovered we both listened to the same Christian program at noon. Together with our bag lunches, we spent each noon sharing lunch while listening to the program. Then we became friends.

Otto became a changed man and never had another angry outburst. I was changed too. In my family, the rule was "don't confront." Reluctantly and fearfully, I followed God's lead and in so doing began to break the Grime family legacy.

God was still maturing me in the ways of confrontation. God chose a woman named Melva at the condo to make his strongest object lesson.

A total and complete terror, she was an iron lady who enjoyed literally raising her fist to rule. Unfortunately she was my next-door neighbor. She garnered strength in controlling everybody and everything. Worse yet, she controlled through manipulation. And, to top it all off, she was quite open about the fact that she did not like Ruth and me because we were Christians.

Once, she had tried to attack Ruth with her cane. A host of daily battles ensued. Typifying them all, she threatened me with legal action if I used my exhaust fan. The reason was she believed I was getting garlic odors in her kitchen.

No one ever resisted because she would enjoy every moment of locking horns. She loved to fight.

What could we do? We invited her to Bible Study. She didn't come.

Ruth discerned we should thank God for Melva. She had run out the people who previously had occupied our condos. It seemed a Godly spin on a difficult situation.

Alas, one day I could stand it no longer. Threatened by her one too many times, with everything in me, I summoned up my courage and said, "Melva, if you don't like it here, why don't you just leave"

She did! In just a little while she moved out of the building and we never heard from her again.

God works in the hard places. A life of prayer does not exclude one from the rigors of life. If anything, life can sometimes be more difficult as one comes in the crossfire of God's transforming ways.

If someone comes to us with an "impossible" situation, we look to where God is going to work. A young man came to our Bible Study with miserable circumstances; no job, an impending divorce, and something about CPS. Ruth declared to him, straight from the heart God gave her, 'We're going to pray you into a job." In two weeks he was employed.

God is always healing the broken places, especially in relationships.

To me there is no such thing as unanswered prayer. It just isn't God's timing yet. He's always working on it. It's just that I can't see it. Sometimes it takes years until we can see an answer. Our 'job' is to keep on praying. It is not ours to wonder about the answers. Focus on dying to your self. If you are not doing that, He will focus on that. Unanswered prayer is not in my vocabulary. The Lord is working on every person. If He's put the words in your heart, then just let it go. Perhaps they're rebelling. It's nothing to be discouraged about. Maybe they're not ready. Maybe they're still working through something.

There were times in the various Bible Studies when strife would tear things. There was one particular situation when a man was, in Ruth's estimation, using the group to reinforce his own personal pity party. Time and time again we would help him out and it would make no difference. Finally she told the group that she thought they should stop helping him. In her wisdom she pointed out we should surely offer emotional and spiritual support but not let him use us financially. She also suggested he see a Christian Counselor. The group discerned her wisdom and together we confronted him. He was very angry that evening and threatened to sue us. We asked him to leave the group. Many people were worried, but Ruth trusted God and sure enough the young man gradually moved away from the group. I have come to rely on Ruth's wisdom in moving through difficult situations.

FIVE
RUTH AND TOM'S PRAYER RELATIONSHIP

"Thank you dear God that it is you which worketh in us both to
will and to do
of your good pleasure. Amen
Philippians 2:13

Ruth:

It wasn't me who accepted Tom; it was God's Spirit in me. For twenty years, I had puzzled through how to talk to him about his issues. My tone could be direct, sometimes harsh. I would tell him, "If you weren't my prayer partner I wouldn't talk to you like this." I was afraid of stunting his growth. I was afraid of enabling him. I was afraid I wasn't allowing him to be himself because I had to initiate almost everything.

Every once in a while, I would tell him I didn't want him in my life anymore.

Tom:

It was real serious stuff. Get lost. Get out of my life. You're just too much. Yelling stuff.

I learned if I just let her say her feelings that it would work out. She just needed to say them. It wasn't as bad as the raging I heard in my childhood.

In battling out our differences, someone else would need prayer. The worst episode came when we stopped talking for a few days. It wasn't first time it happened, but it was definitely the most severe. Ruth was done. She was not going to continue the relationship. The severing went on for several days.

Then a most divine intervention occurred. I still don't remember, or know, why I picked up the phone. It hadn't rung. I wasn't going to call anyone. I wasn't dialing Ruth's number. I simply picked up the phone. Ruth was on the line. Startled to hear each other's voices, we began to talk. It seemed the rift would be healed. Only then did we discover the real miracle. *Ruth had not called me. She had picked up the phone to make another call but she had not dialed my number.* God made clear the purpose of our friendship. Whatever our emotional disparity, our heavenly calling was obvious.

Knowing each other spiritually was to be the gold standard in our relationship. It was not the last rift, but it was the one that defined all others. We looked to the One who made the connection between us. God calls us away from our own problems and back into service. It saved us then and it continues today. Nonetheless, for years, the tension continued.

Ruth:
For me, the relationship was excruciatingly painful. I was driven into the Word night and day. Knowing God would speak to me through the Word and that Tom was trying to heal, I read the verse "...they will soon fade like the grass" and underlined the word *soon*. The strife and Tom's unconscious emotional state was wearing on me.

Despite the reassurance, I couldn't stand the reality. It went on for years. A notation in my Bible marks the frustration after fourteen years. It continued for almost twenty-five years. God's sovereignty is most apparent in the steadfastness of our prayer ministry. We were faithful in our prayers. God would not let us cast aside our ministry because of the void in our emotional bonding. Again and again, God covered the gap.

At one point, I had signed on for a short-term mission. All seemed to be in order and gradually the details unraveled. It became apparent that my reason for the trip was to get away from Tom. It wasn't good enough for God. Doing God's work from a motive of escaping Tom was not an option, so I returned again to the knowledge that I could not escape. God had called Tom and me to prayer.

Tom:
I was trying as hard as ever. I knew intellectually she was telling me the truth. I decided to break the family pattern and not cut and run. I was committed to continuing to try to work it out. Ruth may have been interested in ditching me, but I was not at all interested in getting out of Ruth's life, no matter how angry she was at me.

Eventually there was a concrete example where I could link feeling and action together and observe what I was doing. There was a young woman on a church trip that I did not like and I had specifically mentioned this to Ruth. Yet, repeatedly, I would choose to sit next to her on the bus. Ruth pointed out my behavior compared to my statements. I got it. It was twenty years, but I got it...once. It took several more times. Ruth kept involving me in family events, celebrations, and helping care for her grandchildren. Ruth thought the children might help me forget myself and she was right. She knew I had to start with children to learn to trust. It was very healing. I really love her grandchildren. I am an uncle to them.

Ruth:
God was sustaining us during the whole ordeal. I knew I couldn't quit praying with Tom just because I didn't like him. Tom knew he couldn't quit because it would be falling back into the family pattern. The only reason either of us could quit was if it was getting in the way of our relationship with God and that was not happening. Our prayers were fruitful, so the work continued. There was no sign from God that we should do anything but proceed with the relationship. We were to continue praying together.

Tom:
As if our own internal pressures were not enough, Ruth was also being accused of being a cradle robber. People assumed we were having a romantic relationship and hounded us. If they weren't accusing us of being involved, they were accusing her of being a mother figure. It was very painful. Ruth kept telling me, *"We are not committed to each other. We are committed to prayer."*

It was very hard for me to watch Ruth go through the gossip. I had never had a wholesome, good, in depth relationship with someone before Ruth. Because of God's grace, I knew that Ruth was dependable and trustworthy. It pained me that because of her role in my life, she bore the pain of gossip.

What made it worse, in many ways, was we couldn't understand our own relationship. It was very unconventional. If we couldn't understand it, how could we explain it to somebody else? The personal issues and the spiritual issues had confused us as well as anyone else.

Everyone told us we should not be so close. The hardest part was the criticism from well meaning Christian friends. Even if they didn't always say something, we could feel it.

When we prayed, all of the strain, gossip, and criticism went away. We saw answers to our prayers as well as others. We knew we needed to continue to pray.

The pressure of the gossip was somewhat mediated by our participating in fellowship, although that too presented problems. For Ruth it was a joy, but for me being around people was literally and physically crushing. I had to force myself to be sociable. Ruth thrived being surrounded by others. Outside of the Singles group, family social events were a time when I would just rather go to another room.

In 1990, something happened that provided the turning point I needed. Hard at work in the aerospace industry, I was counting the days until my retirement. I was forty years old and miserable. I could never do enough and always felt like I had to do more.
The engineers at the company have a certain mindset. It's a highly competitive situation for which I was not really suited. Feelings and emotions were a liability.

So many people asked for my help and frequently I could not finish my own work. It was my deepest desire to move to another area so I would not be so accessible to others' demands. I wanted to be able to concentrate on just my own job. Unfortunately I was not allowed to do that. It was like the military. You were assigned a desk and that's where you stayed

One Friday night, Ruth and I were walking around the lake across from the condo, talking about the situation. I was complaining, as usual, about all the things I didn't like about the company. When I mentioned for the umpteenth time that I wanted to move my desk, Ruth called my bluff. She told me to move my desk. I explained a person couldn't do that. She pushed me on it; right into the car. Soon we found ourselves outside the gate of my work. Leaving Ruth in the car I went in with my pass and key and started to go into the building. Suddenly it hit me! "Oh my gosh, I can't do this. Ruth doesn't understand!" I returned to the car. She locked the door and told me if I didn't go do it, she was going to drive home without me.

All the way into the building, all the time I was moving my things to an empty desk around the corner from my group; I couldn't believe I was doing it. All through the weekend I had a sick stomach. True, I had come to realize it *was* what I wanted. But Saturday and Sunday I was in agony.

Monday came and I decided the best thing to do was just act like nothing had happened. My boss, who was a retired general, came in late that morning. Finally the call I'd been expecting came. Would I please come into the bosses' office? When I walked in he was nonchalantly balancing his checkbook. I stood patiently waiting to be fired. To my surprise, the boss talked to me about some inconsequential matter and then dismissed me. He said nothing about my move. In fact nobody said anything the whole day. After so much concern on my part it seemed no one even noticed!

It didn't look like it at first, but that was the beginning of the end. A new boss came and I continued my work as usual, but was soon placed on another assignment. Given my own office and staff, I was supposed to investigate the past practices of the company with regards to disposal of hazardous waste. The company wanted a complete history.

I loved my new assignment and I enjoyed working with my staff, the work itself, and having an office.

The job over, they were going to return me to my group. On a Friday afternoon, I discussed the issue with my supervisor. I pointed out that I enjoyed the freedom and responsibilities. I wanted to continue with similar projects at my current pay level and my supervisor agreed.

On Monday morning, his tone had changed. He told me, in no uncertain terms, the company didn't negotiate with their people. I was to return to my previous little space. Crushed, my anxiety and dissatisfaction began to manifest itself in physical symptoms. My back began to seize and I experienced something like paralysis. It got so bad I couldn't get myself to work. After a few weeks, I left my key and my badge with a note that said, "I'm outa here…"

Ruth:
When he quit, Tom had my full support. I told him I would never let him starve. So began our tradition of eating together. It

also opened the possibility of doing more ministries together. Tom was able to pay more attention to what the Lord wanted him to do. Inner healing, for him, was a gradual awakening. Out from under the emotional burden of the company's climate, Tom began to make giant strides. In the beginning it took him months to register something, then weeks, then days, and now it just takes a little time.

During this time God provided a chance for me to see Tom with his parents. Tom's father came to the Northwest on business. I was actually ill with some cold or flu bug. Undaunted, Tom begged me to go to their hotel with him.

Sick with a fever, I went with him and I was able to see Tom 'disappear' in their presence. It was a startling transformation. He sat and moved as if he was a cardboard cutout; lifeless and void of personal energy. It seemed an automatic response to their very company. It provided deep insight for me into Tom's essential being. This new insight gave me ideas about ways to encourage him.

All along, I knew I did not want Tom to get his identity from me. He needed to get his identity from God. Early on in our friendship, I had discerned that Tom was, on his own, like a spiritual sleeping giant. I knew in my Spirit that, like Ephesians 2:10 points out, "For we are his workmanship, created in Christ Jesus unto good works, which God hath before ordained that we should work in them."

We are still working it out, relying on God's Grace. It is not easy. We no longer have periods of time when we aren't talking to each other, but we do frequently 'clear the decks'. I have learned to endure his behavior to the great end of encouraging his spiritual maturity.

Because of my upbringing, birth order, and God given personality, I am very direct. This directness has sometimes put me at odds with my ethnic roots. I am not your typical Filipino woman. In Filipino culture it is frequently considered rude and offensive to be direct. One of the challenges of being a non-European citizen in the United States is living with racism and, at the same time, a certain distance from one's ancestral heritage. My love for my culture has always outweighed my discomfort.

In college I was always trying to help the Filipino community. In adulthood, I was thrilled when I was asked to join a Filipino chorale especially because I was a music teacher. Much to my chagrin, they didn't reference the written music very often. Without music to read, I just was not able to catch up with them and pick up the groove. Sometimes I could, but most of the time I couldn't. I wanted the group to adhere to the written music. Inevitably there was friction. My background and western ways were clashing with tradition again.

Believing we could work something out, I went to the director and talked about it. Unfortunately, the situation didn't improve. People in the group were irritated by my suggestions and I was frustrated by their unwillingness to follow the written score. It was a contentious situation. Despite the pushing and shoving, the years of being in this relationship helped things to work out. God's hand was reconciling the community to itself every step of the way. We prayed for understanding and peace. Event by event, we kept moving towards each other. By God's Grace we met in the middle.

Now, all has been forgiven. The prayers for understanding and peace have been answered. I kept prayerfully reaching out and God's Grace accepted my grasp. I knew we were of one accord when they asked me to deliver the prayer at the twenty-fifth anniversary celebration of the chorale.

Another opportunity to be in service to the Filipino community did not have such a happy ending. I was asked to teach a Sunday School class for a Filipino church. As many smaller churches do, they were meeting in a facility primarily occupied by a large mainline church.

From the start, there were differences. Time meant nothing to them. They would come late, start late, and behave in what I considered to be a most ill mannered way. It was disrespectful to the hosting church.

I would say to them, "You are in America now. You have to be different about time!" My words had no effect. I felt it was a bad witness for them to inhabit the building without structure or clarity to their time and I told them so repeatedly. Eventually it impacted my life so negatively, I chose to give up the opportunity feeling my efforts were pointless.

Later, I was very embarrassed when the hosting church refused to allow me to have my mother's one-hundredth birthday party at their facility. I found out it was due to the boundary issues the worshipping congregation had incurred.

Most of the time, Tom and I have experienced great victory through the Grace of God and the power of the Holy Spirit. In this instance it was never resolved. Sometimes you just have to let things go.

Working with the Filipino chorale helped prepare me for taking on the largest 'assignment' God ever gave me: the role of devotions chair for my church's choir. After singing with the choir a short while, I was asked to be the devotions chair. As glorious as the fruit eventually was, at first there were some missteps and misgivings.

Being open about situations that need to be prayed for can sometimes make people feel very vulnerable. Some people in the choir did not want their business shared and they didn't want to know other people's business either. They just wanted to sing. The idea of a prayer ministry was very uncomfortable for them.

I sent out a survey as a needs assessment. They told me in writing they didn't like the intrusive nature of prayer requests. Sometimes if I asked a follow up question to a prayer request, I was thought to be nosy or given to gossip. I had to be very careful about sharing. Slowly I learned to walk around the discomfort and lift the prayers in a way that the people recognized as Godly.

Then too it was hard for some people to adjust my style. I am a person with a good sense of humor and few inhibitions. In the beginning of singing with choir, I was comfortable with dressing in flamboyant Halloween costumes during the choir's annual celebration during the rehearsal closest to the holiday. People were shocked and confused. Nevertheless, God graced me with faithfulness, commitment to prayer, and eventually people saw that more than they saw my humorous escapades.

I also toned down a bit in deference to their comfort levels. Once again, the Lord blessed me with an understanding of how to build relationships that would support the growth of prayer. I made a joke when I was assigned to the devotions chair that I was going to 'atone for my sins'. It put people at ease.

Of course, one cute remark could not build trust on its own. That took years of seeing me be faithful to the prayer needs of the choir. Finally most people took me seriously. The Lord was gracious to cover my 'boo boo's'. All along, I knew God would work it for His good.

When I started out, I was not sure how to enact the vision God had put in my heart. I went to the pastor of adult education, at the time. She suggested I start a prayer letter. The venture was going to be exacting. Every week the information would have to be gathered, typed, copied and distributed.

On Sundays, I would gather the prayer requests and praise reports. I always started the letters with praise. On Monday I would start typing them along with a devotional thought. By Wednesday the newsletter had been constructed.

Tom was the courier. On Thursdays he would duplicate the newsletter and put one in each person's box. There were about eighty people in the choir so it was quite an undertaking.

The fruit was worth it. The choir became more like family. People began to share their very real stories. In those stories, the hand of God was apparent. Babies that were born too small and sickly were healed and grew stronger. People with cancer were cured. One man, adopted as a child, found his birth family. People struggling with unemployment found life affirming jobs where they could witness to their faith.

The choir was beginning to define itself as a family. They served each other's needs. A woman whose dear aunt died found herself surrounded with members who put together a memorial service when the extended family had decided none would be arranged. The heart of God pulsed in their care for each other. Private matters evolved into family matters.

A new senior pastor came to the church that, during a workshop with us, put members together in prayer quartets and instructed us to pray together for a year and see what happened. The new relationships brought new trust and a greater revelation of Grace.

Tragedy struck when a member died in a motorcycle accident. We surrounded each other with prayer and made it through. The reality of God's sustaining power in that moment taught us so much about God. We stepped out in faith in our prayers to a deeper level. People started to share more and we continued to pray. The structure of the prayer newsletter provided everyone with an opportunity to respond in emergency situations. We also formed a phone tree.

The Lord gave me the ideas for another dimension of prayer: Choir Angels. A new member would be partnered with an older member. The partnership would begin at the first of the choir year and continue throughout the year. People loved it. We added the idea of a newcomer's luncheon.

After several years, another director came to lead the choir. An ordained pastor, he brought a new depth of faith to the musical experience. Adding a Bible Study, the prayer movement grew. When a long time member was diagnosed with leukemia, one member organized a one hundred-day prayer vigil based on the Psalms. Practical helps abounded; lawn care, meals, and the extravagant gift of flying out of state family members' home for a visit. One family member lived through a stem cell transplant with the support and love and prayers of the whole choir.

As a body, we strengthened our community through prayer. Lifting each other, in increasingly serious difficulties, everyday we saw the fruit of answered prayers. A young couple given the diagnosis their unborn child has a skeletal deformity and has a slim chance of living much past delivery. Not a dry eye was found in the sanctuary the morning he was presented, many months later, for baptism. Rejoicing was the order of the day on his first birthday.

Eventually it was time for me to step down. The computer age had come; the church hired an office assistant. One of the tenors set up a website which allowed prayer requests to be posted and they were sent out automatically every evening to anyone who cared to receive them.

I prayed diligently about my replacement. The answer was obvious. Sara Beth, the young woman whose mother had received a miracle cure for her cancer was the most likely candidate. She is a graphic artist who creates a weekly bookmark size handout of the most recent and on going prayer requests. She and I dubbed her the 'prayer princess'.

The tradition of prayer has grown stronger. Today, each rehearsal has a time of prayer before, in the middle of, and at the end of rehearsal. Whatever the concern, it is taken to the throne, wrapped in thanksgiving and petition and left for God's mighty hand of love and power.

We have become a family who sings together, prays together, share together, studies together, and plays together. It is living proof we learn the most from others. We experience the most active presence of God with others. We serve the Lord most faithfully when we serve others. The most delightful heavenly places are those that are shared. We discovered as a group the love that fuels and energizes the call to prayer.

SIX

RUTH AND TOM'S PRAYER RELATIONSHIP PLUS ONE

Tom's prayer:
"Holy Spirit, thank you for the words
of this Father's Day poem you gave Ruth...
to you whose promises have never failed." Amen

Ruth:

There was a man in the condo named Larry who was a faithful devoted Christian. Tom and I first came to know him as a patient of my eldest son, who is a medical doctor. Eventually Tom began doing bookkeeping for him at the car washes Larry owned. Included within the pictures of the history of my life are some of Larry and his wife Vonda sitting at a holiday meal in my previous house as the guest of my son. He knew they had no family with whom to share the meal and invited them.

Remember when my friend Ruth was sick and I wanted to go to Alaska? Larry was the one who stepped in and pointed out the folly of driving and provided airfare. There were also times we toiled together at condo work parties.

Larry's wife had health issues that made her completely dependent on him. His care for her was impeccable. He did everything including, combing her hair daily. He kept working by taking her with him.

Encumbered with her care around the clock, he sought teaching where he could find it. Since few churches seek out or evangelize shut-ins, television was the place available to him to nurture his Christian beliefs and he soaked up everything he could.

Though our contacts were benign, my reaction to Larry was quite strong. I couldn't stand him. Because of my social nature, my style is encouraging and hospitable. Because of his reclusive nature, his style was didactic and direct. He was very opinionated and tended to lecture more than persuade on the blessings of accepting Jesus Christ as Lord and Savior.

I did my best to avoid him. For someone as confrontive and bold as I am, it was odd to find myself hiding behind cars if I knew he was in the garage. In the midst of it all, I would tell Tom, "We have to love him; he is our brother!"

After Vonda's death, I was increasingly uncomfortable. I found myself struggling with feelings I did not understand. It was hard enough to encounter Larry when his demeanor put me off. Imagine my confusion when I began to discover I was attracted to him.

God works in such enigmatic ways. I have Menier's disease, which results in periods of strong vertigo. The dizziness is so intense that I become nauseous. Each attack is thoroughly debilitating. One evening my condition was so bad, I was desperate. So I had Tom call Larry to see if he could come down and apply his knowledge of reflexology to my feet to see if it would relieve the symptoms.

I was hesitant, but my desire to try anything that would alleviate the symptoms was stronger than either my skepticism or my disdain for Larry. To my amazement, it worked. Larry's massages became routine. When the attacks hit, Tom would summon Larry and the kneading would relieve the dizziness.

Confused and uncertain about my feelings, I made sure Tom stayed with us. He thought it was to protect me from Larry. I knew it was to protect me from my heart. It always sent me into a panic. I didn't want him that close. I didn't understand what God was doing.

Later, Tom remarked to me that Larry liked me and he thought we were flirting with each other. I vehemently denied any such thing and professed to not know what Tom was talking about; at least not that I could admit. After years of me pointing out feelings of which Tom was unconscious, it appeared the shoe was on the other foot.

Inevitably, the day came when my vertigo hit and Tom was not available to call. Left alone, we faced the inevitable.

The truth was we did not like each other, but at this particular time, although our attention was dominated by healing, as we look back now, we seemed to have started experiencing an attraction for each other. When he proposed, I was even more perplexed. It was one thing to fall in love, but getting married again at the age of seventy-eight was something entirely different.

Uncertain, I hesitated. It was not a path I wanted. Tom, for his part, disliked Larry. For him, watching me fall in love with Larry was his worst nightmare. Our prayer ministry was turned upside down. I was unsettled, Tom was in despair, and Larry was delighted. How could God possibly work it for His good? The best and worst chapter of our prayer ministry was beginning.

For three months, I prayed and sought council. Marilyn had a long conversation with me. Just to help me clarify my feelings, Marilyn asked the question, "Why would you want to marry him?" I answered, "Because he tangles with me." By that I meant Larry was equal to the personal power the Lord had given me. I did not intimidate him.

Still unsure, I consulted my friend Joan, a sister in Christ from the choir. She told me to look carefully. It was her opinion this guy was the man for me. I went back and forth. It was a mystery to fall in love and marriage seemed too big a leap.

In the midst of this dilemma, tragedy pushed me to make a decision.

Bea, my niece; my mother's sister's granddaughter, had grown up primarily caring for her younger brothers and sisters. Having shouldered those responsibilities to her best abilities, in adulthood, she became a well-admired teacher. Marriage and children followed. Caught by surprise to find her marriage was in trouble, a divorce soon followed. When the burdens of her life began to become unbearable, I encouraged her to have faith. I shared from the witness of the deep well of faith; to hold onto hope. Bea clung to my faith. I knew it was becoming her own. God was making it so. I taught her a chorus – Something "Bea"utiful, something good. All my confusion He understood. All I had to offer Him was brokenness and strife, but He made something "Bea"utiful of my life. She confessed to me that when she would feel suicidal, this chorus would come to her and she would sing it claiming it as her own – and then she would be able to function as her usual self.

After several years Bea began dating a young man who became her fiancée. At long last she had found true happiness. He was a wonderful man who loved her dearly.

One bright sunny day at the beginning of summer, they went hiking together. As Bea posed for a humorous picture leaning on a stick at an outcropping above a river, her fiancée noticed she was suddenly gone from the viewfinder. Taking the camera down, he discovered she had completely disappeared. Walking to the edge of the outcropping, there was Bea, several feet below pinned under a rock in water he knew to be frigid. The paramedics determined that not only would the impact have killed her, but the icy water added its blow as well. Bea....utiful was gone.... from all of us. It was her nature to care for and love people. We were devastated.

I was suddenly aware of how fragile and tenuous life was. In the midst of the grief, I recognized whatever my own feelings were; it was obvious that it was God's desire for me to be married to Larry. Thinking of God's sovereignty and all that could be lost in a millisecond, I said 'yes'. The next question was when we should get married.

In addition to Bea's loss, I found myself flat on my back with one of the worst episodes of vertigo ever. I also began to hemorrhage heavily from some medication I was taking. Adding to the intensity of my circumstances, Tom and I were scheduled to go to Bosnia the first week in August to work with refugees. It was almost the middle of July. Not only had I changed my life plan by becoming engaged, but also I was now physically incapacitated. I could not see how I was going to be able to go.

With Tom cooking and Larry mopping up after me, I had an opportunity to view my situation in a new way. Watching them work together, God revealed to me the prayer partnership was in His care. Through being forcibly taken out of the picture, God showed me a picture of what the new relationships could look like. I began to look at things from God's perspective once more.

Larry had spoken to me about my prayer partnership with Tom early on. As far as he was concerned, Tom and I were like business partners. He was in full support of our continued partnership. My admonition that Tom and I were committed to prayer together, not to each other was moving to a deeper level.

The crisis of my illness over, people had begun to gather at my place for Bea's funeral. It was impossible to not be incredibly sad. It was a tragic loss of life. The sorrow did not lift for any of us. At the same time, Larry was concerned about my trip to Bosnia. "Anything could happen," he pointed out. He began to press for an immediate marriage. "If I only get to be married to you for two weeks, then it will be worth it," he stated.

What was I to do? Here were sad faces around me and I was dealing with Larry's concerns and my own feelings. I felt inspired by the Lord to take a step.

"OK," I said, "We'll do it! This week! Larry and I will marry by the bench this week!"

The bench is a park bench at the lake near our condo. Tom had heard of a program where people could donate money towards the maintenance of the bench through the parks department. In return, we could place a small placard of dedication on or near the bench. We bought a plaque in honor of my mother.

The plaque quoted a book by Mildred Tanner Andrews, titled: *Washington Women as Path Breaker*, where my mother's graduation photo from Northwest Training School in Seattle was featured. The plaque reads:

Josefa Diaz Barrazona
Path Breaker for...Women Of Color
February 15, 2000

After inquiring and making arrangements, we chose what we thought would be the best of the benches still available. High weeds surrounded it. The program works that the parks department supplies whatever seasonal flowers are left and we do the gardening.

As we got busy clearing the weeds, we were pleasantly surprised to find a lovely rockery, like a mother's cradling arms around the back of the bench. The rocks are low on both sides and come up around it. When everything is in bloom, the bench is somewhat terraced and a thing of beauty. The spot looks out on a small island in the middle of the lake. Whenever we are there gardening, people stop to tell us how much the bench means to them and how they like to look at the rockery and pause at the bench. Many of them sense the area is dedicated to someone special and taken care of by loved ones.

This then, was to be the place for our wedding.

The wedding, with only our nuclear family by the bench, was to be a testament to all that God had ever done for our family.

The bench at Green Lake.

Tom:

I was overwhelmed by the mere thought of Ruth marrying Larry, let alone the reality of it. I kept thinking, "Not Larry! He's repulsive!" It wasn't a matter of what I didn't like about Larry, it was more what *did* I like about Larry? True, I had worked for Larry a little bit by helping him with bookkeeping functions for the car washes he owned, but I couldn't go through with this. My worst fear was to lose Ruth to Larry and that was unthinkable.

To make it worse, Ruth had told me many times that she couldn't go through the marriage without my prayer support. What an untenable position I found myself.

I was also deeply grieving for Bea because we had been very close. So close, in fact, when Bea gave birth to her daughter, I was the one who took her to the hospital.

It was all too much for me to handle and I was not happy at all. I was very angry with God for creating this situation. And then, in the midst of my despair, I opened up my Bible to the book of Ruth. The Lord was saying emphatically, "Larry is Boaz. If he says he's going to do something, he is going to do it!" I started reading it through and saw all the parallels. Ruth and I were Naomi and Ruth. I was Naomi. The Lord revealed to me that Larry was a man of his word.

Larry clearly demonstrated all the trappings of Boaz as a businessman. When he approached me while he was considering proposing to Ruth, he told me, "Whatever I can do to support your prayer ministry; financial, moral, or spiritual, I will do it."

I was angry that I no longer had all of Ruth's attention. However committed I was to prayer, Ruth had played an enormous part in my personal life. Her family had become my adopted family. Losing that closeness was, to me, life threatening. Finding the allegory in the Book of Ruth gave me a framework for moving through the transformation God was setting in motion.

The day of the wedding was wonderful. Impromptu and casual, everything came together nicely. With just family by the bench, Ruth wore a red flowered dress and broad brimmed hat. The little ceremony was deeply meaningful. Everyone's spirits lifted as we looked to the future in the midst of grieving Bea's death.

A couple of weeks after the wedding, there was a *huge* argument. It was inevitable. I referred to it as the clash of the titans. I was very tempted to say, "I told you so, Ruth! Didn't I tell you not to get involved with this guy?" Instead, I found myself praying for them. I knew the prayers had not come from me but from God. I could feel there was something supernatural going on. I kept quiet and didn't say anything.

Praying for them to get back together was very hard to do, because it was the last thing I wanted to do. I was driving up the street in my truck when suddenly it was as if blinders had fallen off my eyes. I could literally feel my peripheral vision increase. The Lord was protecting me from my family all these years and now I don't need these blinders anymore! The Lord spoke to me in my heart. "No good thing will I withhold from you." I didn't know which book in the Bible had the citation. I later looked it up and found it came from Psalm 84:11.

For the Lord God is a sun and shield;
the Lord bestows favor and honor;
no good thing does he withhold
from those whose walk is blameless. (NIV)

The Lord continued, "When you are feeling jealous, when you are feeling left out, remember, I am not holding anything good from you. You're going to get good things."

In one fell swoop God had changed my heart and had taken the blinders from my eyes and reminded me of the good personal future he had for me. As if to underscore instruction with comfort, God led me to open my bible four different times to the same passage (Matthew 8:23-27) describing Jesus calming the storm. I felt so alone and I really needed to hear that God was in the middle of this hurricane.

The final healing would not come for a while, but I had begun to entertain the idea that I might possibly be able to accept their marriage. The battle was in releasing my feelings about my relationship with Ruth.

What I missed was the intimacy. After their marriage, there was a level of sharing that, rightfully so, did not occur between us. Although neither Ruth nor I were interested in or felt any attraction to being married to each other, we had become the deepest of friends.

When Ruth married Larry, again rightfully, he needed to be Ruth's best friend. That left a huge void inside me. However holy, righteous and good it was for this to happen, it was, nonetheless, painful.

The gap appeared in many ways. There were no more times of sharing what the other felt about mutual experiences such as speakers or outings by discussing it after the event. Asking questions like, "What spiritual feeling did you get from that group?" did not happen anymore. These kinds of intimate thoughts needed to be deferred to discussions Ruth had with Larry.

Ruth and Larry began to take trips together and I was left with the visible void of the friendship. Prayer times also changed. Ruth explained that she could not have such an intimate experience as the prayer without Larry present. It was awkward at first working schedules out. Larry's schedule was busy with the car washes. We had to develop new morning routines.

I kept trying but I still had to deal with all of my feelings. I had my marching orders from the Lord but was still struggling to obey. Plus I had begun to worry about what people were going to think at church. If they had gossiped about our friendship before, what would they say about a three-way relationship now? I kept asking the Lord, "what model do I have for this?" and always the answer came back, "Ruth, Naomi and Boaz. Looking back to the previous history of various three-way friendships in our singles group was the predecessor to this relationship. Without knowing it, for years, the Lord had been preparing me and teaching me how to reconcile us to this new situation.

Ruth:

Two weeks after the wedding, it was time to set all the adjustments aside. Tom and I were headed to Bosnia. I had been asked by a friend, Linda Quist, the team leader, months before to pray for people to go on the trip. Sometimes you are an answer to your own prayer!

With our circumstances completely changed, we were going to put legs on our prayers once more and the Lord's protection was evident from the beginning. Days before we were to leave, we were walking in a crosswalk coming home from a jaunt around the lake. Having begun the cross with the green light, we were halfway to the other side when a car running the red light barreled through the crosswalk. To this day, we don't know how he missed us. He drove right by and sped on through, never stopping. The Lord's hedge of protection kept us safe once more.

On the heels of the sorrow of Bea's death and the adventure of my marriage, we discovered getting to Bosnia was going to be one miracle after another. Having been spared from injury or death, we learned our frequent flyer miles were going to completely cover the round trip. It would cost us nothing to get there and back!

When we began making travel arrangements, we learned there were no seats available. The agent was very firm about that. Tom explained why we needed to fly then because we were going to a Bible camp. The comment prompted the agent to talk to her supervisor and see if anything could be done. The next day she called back and we had our seats. We were on our way!

It took hours by bus to get to the camp. The Bosnians had a phobia about germs in the air making them sick. With the temperature in the eighties, the windows on the bus remained closed for twelve hours.

Once there, we found the ministry opportunities were rich. All the years of helping refugees and my personal experience of being a refugee came together in the days of ministering to them. I discovered there were some Folk Loristic dancers there. One of the women had a filthy towel that she used when she danced. I gave her a beautiful scarf and it transformed her.

The most difficult part was trying to figure out where they were all coming from emotionally. They had gone through two years of war isolated in their basements. This camp was the first chance for them to get out of their homes. They were on holiday and we spent a lot of time trying to figure out their needs so we could help and serve them.

One man came with many questions about Christianity and I encouraged him to ask all the questions he wanted. By the end of the time, he was not as negative about Christianity and had begun to be open to the idea. The luxury of camp was the opportunity to form strong relationships in a short time.

As with any trip, it wasn't perfect. Some of the indigenous leadership felt we weren't doing substantial enough spiritual activities with the campers and were critical of us for that reason. But the people we came to help loved us and we loved them back. We felt the relationships we made were very important.

We did, in fact, have all kinds of activities including a woman's group where we would take turns teaching each other various skills. I was teased a lot about being a newlywed. Beyond the teasing, I shared my own experiences as a refugee and a minority in America. I hoped my testimony had meaning beyond the words. The very fact I was present proved I had survived the refugee experience and I hope was an encouragement.

Tom:

Back home, Ruth's family had begun to adjust to her married status. One of Ruth's daughters had never accepted me in the entire time of our friendship and it was extremely hard on me. That all changed with the marriage. Not only did she embrace Larry as her father, but she also directed new words of affirmation and kindness towards me as her brother, at one point telling me I was a real asset to the family. Two friends from choir decided Ruth and

Larry needed to celebrate the wedding with the choir and other church friends. It was too momentous an occasion to be left at the bench. And so the plan for a second wedding began.

Poem written by Ruth for Fathers' Day, June 20, 2004.

To Larry, my beloved husband, and to Tom, a loyal friend and prayer partner of thirty years:
Greetings on this day reserved to celebrate all Fathers)

In the mystery of His sovereignty,
You both have been gifted NOT only to me!
Only in the Wisdom of the Ages
Had He placed both of you in our family.

You took the position of friend and FATHER
So natural, without even trying.
Giving me a stability, being their mother.
Restoring joy and peace beyond understanding!

The cup getting more full, beyond our expectations
Daily being filled as we focus on thanking
The One whose life was unpretentous,
The Way, the Truth and the Life, all encompassing!

Today, our celebration includes all
Who contributed in some small or large scale
Passed on and living, those who heard the call
To purpose-driven lives, Also to them: All Hail!!!

Gratefully yours, Ruth Norton

SEVEN
GOD IS GOOD

Ruth's prayer:
"Like your first miracle at a wedding when you changed water into wine, you have started to continually change Larry, Tom and I. Thank you! Amen

*T*hey had gone shopping for a wedding suit. Although they found one perfect for the occasion, Ruth could not imagine wearing other than her native dress for such a definitive event. Her long, pale green gown with the signature butterfly sleeves of the Filipino cultural dress radiated peace and joy. The sleeves, constructed by inserting a lining through them that stiffens them, balanced her impeccable posture

  Surrounded by the cathedral choir, their friends and family, they spoke their vows. Tenors and basses and sopranos and duets and quartets provided musical benedictions to the ultimate purpose of the day.

Seattle Yacht Club: Wedding reception given by the Cathredral Choir.

The speeches were beginning. Ruth's children spoke as witnesses to the radiance of her happiness with Larry. Friends attested to each other of God's clear presence in the divine calling of this union. Finally Larry began to speak.

With a piece of paper visibly shaking in his hands he began to speak of the joy of finding Ruth. **He began, "All of you are here today helping us to thank God and celebrate the gift that He has given Ruth and I to each other. Some of you know that since my wife died two years ago, I have been without a biological family."**

He paused. Opening his mouth again to speak, he found the joy had overwhelmed him with tears. He took a moment to gather his composure. **"I also have not had the experience of being in a spiritual family. Since I married Ruth, she now shares with me four children and ten grandchildren plus others she has adopted. As I have observed the way this event unfolded up to the present, I am increasingly being aware of the awesome Heavenly Father who made us One Family. Thank you for being here to demonstrate this to me. I love you all!"**

Ruth:

After a lifetime of praying for others, it would be impossible, according to God's economy, to not have had a myriad of circumstances showering us with blessings of friendship, good fortune and healing. It's been said, don't ever pray for something for someone else that you don't want for yourself.

God's activity had been evident in each of my children's lives. For all the times God called me to service, He poured down blessings on each of them. There were some times my children were not as supportive of my faith and ministry. For a time, we were alienated causing great pain for me. Tom was the source of encouragement during those times. Daily we prayed for reconciliation. Today, through the grandchildren, hearts have been melded and family functions are joyous occasions.

My oldest son was blessed when he applied for medical school. The school completely rewrote their admissions requirements to admit him as the first Filipino student in a culture where traditionally only the doctor's son or wealthy white men were admitted. Twice, once in 2000 and again in 2004, he was honored as one of the top ten doctors in the city of Seattle. The latest accolade comes with the honor of being named an "Asian American Living Pioneer for his contributions to the local Asian community and the health-care profession."

My other son was scheduled to have breakfast at the World Trade Center the morning of September 11, 2001. For some reason, he altered his schedule that morning and that spared his life.

Many opportunities have presented themselves to pray for my relatives outside America. One niece living in Canada still credits our prayers with changing the heart of their church. They were having a struggle with lifelessness in their church. The pastor was not allowing the Spirit to flow freely. I went and visited and after prayer we waited to see what God would do. On his own, the pastor decided to leave. The church is now enjoying a surge of renewal. Recently Larry and I visited on the occasion of the death of one of the family. I again reminded them to find comfort and peace in the reading of scripture; most especially in the Psalms. It is my privilege to point always to the goodness and sovereignty of the Lord.

One relative in the Philippines was brave beyond measure. The story of God's intervention and protection in her life is a book in itself. Her mother and I had grown up together. Her mother was an orphan and my family informally adopted her. We sent her to school and we were all quite close. Eventually during WWII she got married, had children and our families lost touch.

When contact was renewed, one of the things Tom and I did to help was to give their village money to establish a piggery. With that, they could have some self-sustaining income. In the process of doing that, we discovered they didn't have a local source of water. They were traveling miles a day to fetch water and bring it back to the village. We gave them the resources to dig a well and construct a water tank.

We also experienced the joy of giving them the money to send one particular daughter to school, Acsa Raminez. She graduated and began to work for Land Bank of the Philippines. She was a cashier and in that position she found discrepancies where thousands of dollars of tax money was routed to personal accounts. She went to her superiors and was immediately suspected of being responsible. After much prayer, seven years of investigation, authorities concluded she had nothing to do with the shortages.

By that time, however, her life was in danger from those who *were* responsible. She hid her small children in the rural areas with her mother and sisters and only saw them on weekends. This went on for years and she was in agony. Eventually, the bank gave her a bodyguard for safety. She was able to move to a guarded community. Almost all of the media in Manila rallied behind her when she was "blackballed."

True to his commitment to be part of our prayer ministry, Larry joined us in helping her with getting her water fixed and getting a fence around her own house. Larry took my family as his own. Everyone involved prayed...endlessly. Because of prayer, not only was she protected in a dangerous situation, but she also was invited to the presidential palace for lunch. The President, Gloria Arroyo, issued a formal apology and notation of gratitude for uncovering an enormous ring of fraud!

When, several months later, she was approached by a presidential candidate for an endorsement because of the common knowledge of her integrity, she again held her ground in the face of worldliness. She declined the offer and dedicated her steps to praying for the candidate that was God fearing.

Throughout the history of the Philippines, Tom and I, and now Larry, have prayed for that country during times of political upheaval. We have repeatedly seen God answer their and our prayers in mighty ways. Only recently, we were notified of a forty-day prayer commitment as the Philippines moved to elect a new president.

One of the longest prayer burdens we ever had was for a female relative suffering under more oppression than it would seem God could deliver her from. Born out of wedlock, the mother transferred her hatred for the father to the daughter. He had deceived her and committed bigamy by marrying her.

Physically and emotionally abused, this woman was in a dysfunctional marriage for twenty plus years. Three children came from this union. Finally railing against it all, she divorced and became entangled with men who were much younger than she. She also got involved with drugs and spent some time in jail. Her body caving in on itself, she was diagnosed with heart disease and cancer. It got to the point we were never sure if what she was saying was true. Our successive Bible Studies prayed for her continually. Once, prompted by the Spirit, Tom and I drove hundreds of miles without stopping except to change drivers to see her. We arrived to find her in the hospital after a suicide attempt. Having discussed the situation with the social worker, we brought her to our home where she was enveloped with love and care and spiritual healing. Unfortunately her boyfriend followed her. She returned with him and continued her destructive lifestyle. She became alienated from her children to the extent that she was not even invited to her only daughter's wedding.

Persistently, we prayed for her. Ten years passed.

In a transformation that can only happen by the Lord's hand, she found her way to a charity rehabilitation program. She became the director of a similar program for others. Reconciled with her family, she recently took time off from work to help her daughter with her newborn baby. What a joy it was to visit her recently and see her vitality and enthusiasm for life. She is living evidence of the blessing of the Holy Spirit at work. It is that presence that is our greatest reward. The lives we have witnessed changed, not by might or by power but by the Spirit, and that is the sustaining force in our prayer ministry.

Tom:

The Lord had been working in both our families for many years. My sister and I shared a poignant moment together when our mother was dying.

She being the oldest in the family, she was also the outcast. I've mentioned before when she was born, our parents were overwhelmed. A year later when my twin sister and I were born they were not prepared. Since my parents had few social resources for asking or receiving help, my sister paid the price. For one year of her life, the first year, she was actively loved. Then there was just not enough energy.

After I became a Christian, the Lord did a lot of intervening for me to become close to her and say, "We treated you badly." During our mother's last days, although there was no incentive for me to visit my mother, I began to encourage Connie to visit her in the hospital. Before I allowed the Lord to completely transform me, I tried to coerce Connie into a final visit with Mom. Ruth called me on it and told me to leave it alone. Seeing the wisdom in her statement, I did. Thankfully, my sister decided on her own that we should take a trip together to the hospital.

There was at least a foot of snow on the ground when I arrived on the East Coast. . The distance from picking up my sister to the hospital was several hundred miles. We didn't know exactly where we were going. As usual, the Lord guided us there.

I don't know how she ever had the strength or the willingness to go. When Connie came in through the door, my mother, who did not suffer from any dementia said, "Who is that person?" To the end she would not acknowledge her own daughter. Denying her all her life, she continued on her deathbed.

I don't know how my sister took it, but she did. When she left, she bent down to kiss mom on the cheek. My mother turned her face away. That's how it ended. My sister was totally devastated. It took all her energy just to leave the room and get downstairs. Making it all the more devastating, my mother died on Connie's birthday.

I saw God's Grace in my sister's life. Even though she might not call it the same thing, it's very tangible in her life.

The next time we visited, Ruth and I were able to share a small parable of God's provision and care. My sister's partner had been looking for river rocks. Ruth loves to look for rocks so we all piled into the van we had rented at the last minute. It so happened that the interstate was being rebuilt, leaving many rocks by the side of the road. In the grandest of rides, we scooted along picking up rocks to the delight of my sister's partner.

Ruth:

It has been said many times it is impossible to out give God. If the Lord returns twofold for every act of faithfulness, we were due for a harvest of blessings. The questions one could ask are many. What would it look like when the harvest began? Would the blessings be recognizable to them as blessings? How would it change our ministry?

Five years after I purchased my condo, Tom was able to purchase his in the same building. Another remarkable story of God's provision, in one weekend's time, God revealed twenty thousand dollars for Tom to make the purchase. It seemed somehow 'balanced' in God's economy that my son moved in to my house when I moved into the condo, and my daughter moved into Tom's houseboat. God blesses us with the ability to bless others with our resources.

From the beginning we have prayed the condo would be a lighthouse for the Lord. At first it was very difficult. I planted rose bushes and trees in the parking strip outside my condo window and people complained, but I persisted. The Lord gave me many ideas for building community. I organized the tenants to clear a rockery behind the building. I brought them together for meals and holidays. Slowly, their attitude began to change. People who weren't supportive moved away. Those who stayed drew closer. The Lord was working things out for His glory.

As concrete as the blessings coming our way have been, we both define a blessing and gift as simply walking in the Spirit. As much as our story is about prayer, it is equally about an ever-maturing relationship with the Spirit.

Tom:

Truly, a blessing is having evidence of the Holy Spirit. "Being blessed is being at the right place and time doing what we are meant to do" was a sermon by Earl Palmer, the former Senior Pastor at our University Presbyterian Church. Sometimes, it 'feels good'. The Spirit is inspiring, leading, orchestrating, empowering, changing, uplifting and brings life and hope in and through events; the evidence of things hoped for and things not seen. The Spirit brings whatsoever is good, honest and of good report.

Sometimes, however, it doesn't 'feel good'. When the Spirit convicts, not condemning, but encouraging us to confess a sin by talking to someone about it, change a bad habit, or face the truth.

The arrival of Larry on the scene has been the biggest faith challenge I have experienced since 1975 when I accepted Jesus as my Lord and Savior. Nine months after they were married, I was able to sit down and tell Larry I was jealous of him. It opened the door to the two of us having our own relationship. The marriage has become an avenue of opportunity for all of us to grow and change. A little over a year into the marriage, after returning from a trip to Israel, Ruth sat me down and told me it was time for us to have separate meals. Again, the force of the change hit me with a perilous power. Again, the Lord's promise was trustworthy. I discovered, left to my own schedule, I had more time to get things done. It's another example of how the Lord uses bad news or something I was against into something that would be very good for everyone involved.

It is reminiscent of the way in which the Lord led me to enjoy the hustle and bustle of the church activities I encounter in my ushering duties. It's taken years, but now I'm really enjoying being around the people and the demands. I can begin to relate to them and not lose my identity.

The same applies to the situation with Larry. Initially it was something I was against and was threatening. Now the Lord has turned it to something positive. God shows up best in weak people. He will use that weakness for his advantage and your blessing.

The most remarkable life change for me has been the ability to speak in public. Recently, I was asked to be a witness during the worship service to the joys of ushering. The little boy who hid under the bed when people came over was transformed into a man comfortable with speaking in front of thousands of people.

When the opportunity arose, I had no choice. I had to let go and cling to God. I saw all the work the Lord had done in me with regards to my personal life, my relationship with Ruth and the adjustment to the marriage. I could not say no.

God's desire will become yours and that is truly being contented, fulfilled, and at peace. I simply want to be obedient to and for Him. I do not want to miss the opportunities and blessings He has for me.

The Sunday I witnessed happened to be the Fourth of July. It was indeed my independence (from the dead things of the past) day.

Ruth:

I believe the prayer ministry has saved me from several marriages and divorces. I just know that would have happened if the

Lord hadn't led me to a life of prayer. This is the value of praying with someone for a long time. People get in and out of relationships. They don't stick with it and lose a lot. It's like planting a seed. When the insects come, you have to spray them away. It takes a while for the seed to grow. Then it blooms and it is such a blessing. If you are called to God's service, it's a wonderful experience to behold. There is no formula to follow. There are no rules to the way. If you are thinking of finding a prayer partner, pray about it.

In the years since our marriage, Larry and I have grown deeply at the hand of the Lord. It took us almost two years to trust each other and be comfortable in discussing our beliefs. Larry admits he is still working on this trust. We just have to trust Him.

We have discovered common doctrinal beliefs: salvation is by faith not works; the Holy Spirit instructs; our strong beliefs in the power of prayer; in humility Grace abounds; and equal submission for all.

Larry's prayer request from the onset of joining our prayer ministry has been for "God to allow him to have a complete makeover." Our small group and other prayer partners, such as Virginia, are faithful in praying for us.

The Lord gave me the wisdom to insist on spending as much time with him, without suffocating him, and give him the liberty to set his limits. Since there are still rough edges to his commitment for a new phase in his life, I remind him his prayers are being answered.

For a year, we went to counseling. When our counselor suggested a program contradictory to Biblical principles, we switched to a Christian counselor. It was like breathing fresh air. He had us read Proverbs daily and started us on the book, "Every Women's Desire: Every Man's Guide to Winning the Heart of a Woman" by Stephen Arterburn and Fred Stoeker with Mike Yorkey. With the backing of scripture to their words, we were led in the reading of it to understand new concepts of submission. My secret prayer request was that the Lord help me put up with everything about Larry that I didn't like. There was an intense short period of darkness and gloom until we started to read the book. Our prayers have definitely been answered. We now know how to support each other. I often quote II Corinthians 13. *"The first word in the definition of Love is patience."*

Recently our whole family gathered for my granddaughter's wedding. There in that room with hundreds of people sharing our joy, was the evidence of all the relationships healed by God's hand through our prayers over the years. The lavender and deep purple color scheme reflected the deep power of God's love. Gathered in that place were family members who, by all rights ought to have been alienated. God had drawn us all together in his infinite wisdom that we might encourage each other and celebrate who God had made us to be. Old wounds were washed clean and healthy hearts were everywhere. It was possible that night to see clearly who we all would have been had not the power of prayer moved through our family. It was a night of great celebration. It was a witness to all that God can do, if we seek the heart of God and pray the words He places in us.

Tom:
We have always believed that the Lord had called all three of us together to pray and see what and where the Lord was leading and preparing us to do. It was challenging, difficult, and sometimes downright painful. The term "dying to yourself" took on an entirely new meaning for each of us.

Ruth:
A big breakthrough came in January, 2006 when we were in Palm Desert, California where we had a "chance" meeting with my nephew and niece Benny and Olga Quinones. He had been working at World Bank and at the United Nations, helping Third World countries develop their own economies. Benny had always hoped he would be able to carry the same economic and inherent Christian principles he had used in earlier programs for his native Philippine Islands.

It was during these talks that our Foundation was conceived and commitments made to fund and organize a non-profit, tax-exempt international organization. On April 13, 2006, On Eagle's Wings Foundation was born. Larry called the creation of the Foundation a spontaneous manifestation.

Three months later, Larry and I bought a three-story townhouse and moved away in December from our condos at Greenlake.

Because our new home had a spacious basement, Tom moved in with us. This was another step of faith for all of us to try to live together; previously we had our own condos.

Ruth's Final Thoughts:

There are always many reasons to give up. You're going to get bumped here and there. Opposition is a given. Know that God has put you up to it and He will see you through. When God is calling, physical or spiritual pain does not matter. He can get you through those things.

How To Pray:

I asked Ruth how to pray. Is there a right or wrong way? At first, Ruth said, "I can't tell you how to pray." But upon further reflection:

Ruth:

It's spiritual, not human and more power than physical. The bottom line is desire. If you are sincere, the Holy Spirit will pull you in. That's how everything starts. It's simple. Give yourself to God's hand.

Talk in a normal conversation like with your best friend, only it's God. Don't use flourishes, remember who you are addressing. It's a privilege to be talking to Him. No need to feel, think, or be formal.

Start with praise and thankfulness. Admit your shortcomings. Essentially, you are clearing the decks with God. Have a heartfelt conversation and allow God to speak more than you do. Don't worry about a time frame; your conversation can be brief or long. Be open.

Faith says he will answer and why wouldn't He? He always does, but He can answer in unexpected ways. Sometimes we are the answers to our own prayers.

Get involved praying and soon you are really involved. Let the Lord show you the opportunities.

Afterword:

The amazing journey they have taken both separately and together demonstrates the sheer power of God's love. For me, writing their life story has opened my eyes in many ways. Ruth and Tom are two of the most wonderful people I have ever met and the time we've spent together has shown me honest love, caring, and the power of prayer. Professionally, I started as a writer in training, but since I've started working on IN HIS NAME, my writing life has exploded. I now review for the Associated Press and several magazines. I have published a reference book and have written a couple of novels. Without their guidance and prayer, I would not be the person I am today. I thank the Lord every day for placing them in my path.

About the Author:

Jeff Ayers has had the pleasure of knowing Ruth and Tom for over 15 years. He's the author of Voyages of Imagination: The Star Trek Fiction Companion (Pocket Books, 2006) and has written reviews and articles for the Associated Press, Library Journal, the Seattle Post-Intelligencer, and Writer Magazine, among others. He lives, reads, writes and prays in the Pacific Northwest.

Made in the USA
Charleston, SC
04 November 2012